# FROM SNICKET TO WICKET

**David Mitchell**

Published by New Generation Publishing in 2018

Copyright © David Mitchell 2018

First Edition

**www.newgeneration-publishing.com**

 New Generation Publishing

*Dedicated to Peter. Thanks for your interest and motivation*

***Cricket*** - *The game which has developed from white-clad players using a red ball to red-clad players using a white ball.*

# Acknowledgements

***Thanks to***

*Eric Mitchell, Settle's legendary number three, for allowing the use of some images from his own collection.*

*Adrian Braddy, editor of 'Dalesman' magazine, for kindly featuring a series of three items from the book in the magazine during Spring 2018*

*Back cover image shows Settle Cricket Club.*

# Contents

1 Casting an eye over the game ........................................... 1

2 The day Norman O'Neill nearly put me in hospital ...... 4

3 Boundaries at Bond Lane ............................................... 6

4 If it's good enough for Bradman… ............................... 7

5 Wickets down the Snicket ........................................... 11

6 Settle Cricket Club ...................................................... 14

7 'Tally-wagging' ........................................................... 19

8 School Cricket ............................................................. 23

9 Cricket Festivals ......................................................... 29

10 The games people play ............................................... 32

11 My admiration for Sir Geoffrey .................................. 36

12 The Pink ...................................................................... 40

13 College Cricket ........................................................... 42

14 League Cricket ............................................................ 44

15 Friendly Cricket .......................................................... 58

16 Cricket Equipment ...................................................... 59

17 Scoring ........................................................................ 64

18 Captaincy .................................................................... 67

19 Life On Tour ............................................................... 71

20 Televised Cricket ........................................................ 74

21 Watching Test Cricket Live ........................................ 78

22 Test Match Special ...................................................... 84

23 Shipping Forecast ....................................................... 86

24 The Scorecard Seller ...................................................... 87

25 Playing on the outfield ................................................ 89

26 Beach Cricket ............................................................. 91

27 Overseas Players ......................................................... 94

28 Putting a Spin on it ..................................................... 97

29 Doing the Double ....................................................... 100

30 Favourite international cricketers ............................. 102

31 The Consummate County Cricketer ......................... 104

32 A Wisden Schools Eleven 1974 ............................... 106

33 Cricket Pavilions ....................................................... 108

34 Umpires ..................................................................... 109

35 Scarborough in Winter ............................................. 111

36 Taunton in Summer ................................................... 113

# 1  Casting an eye over the game

I have a problem when passing cricket grounds. I just have to steal a glance, particularly if there is a game on, and my attention is immediately taken. The length of that glance depends on the circumstances. Obviously it is easier if I am walking. Then I can stop and absorb as much detail as I wish, even take a photograph. I will look at the scoreboard. What does it reveal about the state of the game? What can I tell from fielding positions? I might have played on the same ground at one stage or possibly even know a player or two. Equally, I could well be absorbed by the activities and movements of players who are unknown to me on a green piece of England a couple of hundred miles from home. It will be an unfamiliar corner of England yet a reassuringly familiar scene. There will be a mixture between experience and youth. The older guys in the visiting team will have provided the transport as well as many a tale of past encounters.  The younger ones will not yet have banked a store of memories and, for the time being, will have turned away from the many distractions of modern life. How long will that last for? The lures of weekend jobs, activities with friends and the internet are some of many rival attractions for their time. There will be a clutch of loyal spectators on the boundary edge and cars parked far enough away to avoid a mighty hit crashing through the windscreen. Inside the pavilion a small group will be making busy preparing the teas. Nearby, the urn will be bubbling towards a crescendo somewhere around the end of the first innings.

The merest hint of a glance has to suffice if I'm at the wheel. Match…road…match…road. If I'm lucky I have timed my passing perfectly and I can see a ball being bowled or a shot made. If the bowler is walking back to start his run, the risk becomes too great. I want to know what happens but might just be denied. A glance back in the rear view mirror may reveal the outcome of that delivery. A late fielding change or a fastening of a bootlace can spoil the moment and I am left unfulfilled. I drive on. There will be another chance another day, maybe even further down the road in the next village.

Even in winter, my gaze will drift across a ground. There might be leaves strewn across the outfield, maybe a score on the board left over from the last game of the season. My mind instantly conjures up images of figures dressed in white acting out a match. I will feel sentimental and nostalgic. Some might call it barmy but this is how cricket can affect you. There is no finer game to watch or play and I consider myself fortunate to have enjoyed both.

There is no other sport to match cricket from a social point of view. Football and rugby finish earlier and after pie, pickle and pint it is time to go. With cricket, the later finishes tend to preclude other activities in the evening so people stick around more, drink in hand, reminiscing with the opposition. Cricketers have an amazing capacity to recall details about games. In their normal life they likely forget birthdays and anniversaries but they can give chapter and verse on the tied game in 1993 or the time Fitz took nine wickets and was denied all ten by a run out. The fund of stories is unrivalled.

Cricket has formed a backcloth to my life since childhood. As I write it appears that the white ball versions could take a stranglehold. Red-ball cricket is suffering by comparison. In February 2018 it was announced that Adil Rashid was only going to play white-ball cricket for Yorkshire in the coming season, at his own instigation. The county fulfilled their side of the bargain only for Rashid to be selected once again by England for a Test match! The balance is in danger of tipping out of control as the game looks to market alternatives which appeal to the modern audience and bring in big money from advertising and sponsors. That staple of my childhood, adolescence and adult life, the County Championship, is under threat.

I find myself longing more and more for past seasons where there was a familiar feel to the fixture list. County

Championship games would take place throughout with Test matches and Gillette Cup fixtures interspersed. I know that it cannot happen. Cricket has to compete to survive. However, nothing can stop me reminiscing about the part that this great game has played in my life, right back to the age of six when it first made its mark. The location was Bradford.

## 2 The day Norman O'Neill nearly put me in hospital

I watched my first live cricket at Bradford Park Avenue in May 1961, days before my seventh birthday. It could easily have been my last. The game was between Yorkshire and Australia. There hadn't been a ball bowled on day one. Watching the action with me was my cricket-loving Grandad, Walter. We had got to the ground by train and bus from Skipton. Grandad Mitchell was a good player in his time. He turned out for Skipton in the local leagues. His gnarled hands bore evidence of a career behind the stumps and he regaled me with stories of broken bones and cricketing exploits. He once kept to the great West Indian Learie Constantine, you know. Cricket had run through previous generations. My great-grandfather was obsessed with the sport, along with angling. If he did not turn up for a match at Skipton, someone ran along the canal bank to find him. He was always there. No respectable salmon reach for him but the often murky waters of the Leeds-Liverpool canal. Grandad's uncle had played the odd match for Yorkshire but apparently didn't get on with Lord Hawke, the Yorkshire and England cricketer who was actually born in Lincolnshire.

Yorkshire's team facing Australia wasn't a hybrid mixture of reserves and promising youngsters like you might get today in tourist games. These were games to be won. There was pride at stake and the big guns would be selected. The team sheet for the game read: Bryan Stott, Brian Bolus, Doug Padgett, Brian Close, Phil Sharpe, Ray Illingworth, Vic Wilson, Don Wilson, Fred Trueman, Jimmy Binks and Bob Platt. A month later, Trueman and Illingworth faced the Aussies in the First Test at Edgbaston. Australia were treating the game as important preparation for the upcoming Test series.

4

Bill Lawry was about to make his Test debut at Birmingham. Grandad and I watched him open up with a partnership of 66 with Bobby Simpson before he was bowled by Platt for 29. Neil Harvey came and went. The eye-catching contribution came from Norman O'Neill who batted at four. Dubbed the 'new Bradman' he never fulfilled that demand but he had astonishing power all the same. He certainly left his impression on Grandad and me on that May day in Bradford.

As we left the ground O'Neill was sixty not out and Australia would declare the next day when he reached 100. His innings was full of memorable shots. I still remember him launching into a pull shot at the Football Stand End. Grandad and I were sitting just behind square. I saw the ball come on to the bat and, seconds later, it crashed into the crowd, just several seats away from us. There was no time to react. Hit a second earlier and I was heading for Bradford Infirmary. It was a moment in time which fuelled my interest in cricket. For Grandad, responsible for my welfare that day, it was quite a shock. For me, it was the most exciting moment of my short life so far. I played it down when I reported back to Mum and Dad that evening but I was eager for more! Mum's main issue was that I had brought the wrong jumper back, leaving Granny's new hand-knitted one at the ground. A decade and a half later I was to play a couple of seasons at Bradford Park Avenue, batting on that same square as Norman O'Neill.

# 3 Boundaries at Bond Lane

It must have been soon after that I began to play the game. I was in the juniors at Settle Primary School. In the summer we had lessons outside and went on nature rambles. Playground games centred around various forms of tig and the ultra-violent British Bulldogs. Bulldogs was banned when an unfortunate pupil put his head through a section of the garage which was sited along one edge of the playground.

Each week our class wound its way, crocodile-style, through the streets of Settle. The destination was Bond Lane playing fields just below the railway station. Mr.Plumridge led as we left the school behind. His bald head glinted in the sunshine at the head of the crocodile of kids. We walked down School Hill past the Folly, turned left at the bottom towards the Police Station, across Duke Street, down Station Road, past the railway station, under the bridge and through a small gate set in a wall. These days you would need to fill in ten pages of Health and Safety forms to do that and have it approved by the School Governors. For those of us who had any energy left we ran on to a grassy area which formed the site for our games lessons. And it was there that I was introduced to cricket. It was pretty basic stuff with limited equipment but it was fun. We had to allow time to make the return journey, this time uphill, so sessions were never lengthy. It was a start, though, and I was hooked. That priceless tract of greenery will never dim from my memory. It is somehow reassuring to know that the tiny gate in the wall has stood the test of time. It serves as my equivalent of the route to Narnia through the back of the wardrobe.

# 4 If it's good enough for Bradman...

With the arrival of cricket in my life our modest back garden took on a whole new significance. In that small space I began to hone the all-round skills that would, one day, result in selection for England. Hadn't the greatest Test batsman of all time started out in the most basic of ways by hitting a golf ball against a rainwater tank with a cricket stump? If Don Bradman could do it, so could I. My tools were a hairless tennis ball and a cheap bat with a ripped grip. With a bit of creativity I was able to transform the back yard of 4, High Hill Grove into my very own cricket academy.

The wall that backed on to number five was covered in pebbledash. The effect of throwing the ball at it was twofold. It came off at unpredictable angles, which I wanted, and took off pieces of the stonework, which Mum and Dad didn't want. I had to build fielding sessions in while they were distracted. It was the simplest but best way to develop catching ability and with my large hands catching a ball soon became second nature. Years later, when I went into teaching, I urged young cricketers to practise with a 'ball and a wall'.

The pitch was a straight but narrow concrete path which led up to the back gate. It wasn't a perfect surface. Cracks were evident in a way that they might be on day five in the West Indies. On either side, and a few inches higher, were raised strips of 'lawn', for want of a better term. Let's say that I wouldn't have liked to face Fred Trueman on it. Taking my stance at the opposite end of the path to the gate, I started to hit the ball up and down the narrow strip. Ideally, it struck the stone step below the gate square on and headed off back in my direction. Each time, I repeated the shot without the need to pick the ball up. It took a while to properly master it. Accuracy was vital to keep the routine going and progress could be halted as it landed on the grass, in the neighbour's garden or on the back road. Occasionally, I substituted the tennis ball with a ball which bounced excessively. These were popular at the time and available from Speight and Watsons on Duke Street. I think they were called Super Balls and so many of my friends had them. They were made of a much harder material and were far more difficult to control but I could begin to imagine the West Indian attack of Wes Hall and Charlie Griffith coming

In the back garden with bat and snake belt

at me. This was a much greater challenge and ran the risk of breaking a window if the ball went out of control.

In the direction of the covers, the grass merged into a small concrete area. I suppose you would call it a patio these days. I'd never heard of the word back then. Next to it was the coal bin, round about gulley. My sister Janet or I would sit on this and count the coal bags delivered each week for Mum and Dad, making sure that the right number were dropped in.

I soon got the hang of my back yard game and the gradual drop in level from the gate to my batting position gave added momentum as the ball came back time and again. I did not need any human help. My goodness, I must have struck the ball thousands and thousands of times. I would work my way through the Yorkshire batting order. Each time I was out I walked disconsolately into the house through the back door before re-emerging as the next batsman, confident and determined. I batted left-handed when I was Brian Close or Don Wilson. With Close I tucked the bat in tight to my body, exaggerated the bend in the torso and stuck my chin out defiantly. I stopped short of copying Close's hairstyle, mind. There were limits. Wilson, born within a mile of where I lived, stood tall with cap at a jaunty angle and swung more freely. There were no helmets in those days so I was spared using Dad's from his motor bike. I built up entire innings in my imagination, working through the Yorkshire line-up as they faced Lancashire at Headingley or Old Trafford.

When one or other parent was available I set up differently. Now I was able to bat at the top end with the gate as wicket. Mum and Dad offered contrasting bowling styles. Mum was a decent cricketer, having played for Johnson and Johnson's factory at Gargrave years ahead of Rachel Heyhoe-Flint's era. Mum paced a run-up back to the living room window and bowled a tidy right arm medium which more than kept me on my guard. Dad was a left arm bowler whose style could best be described as busy. An outhouse prevented him from coming in over the wicket. A box of matches rattled in his pocket as he ran in to bowl and, as a chain smoker, his spells were necessarily shorter in length. It was my first introduction to a varied bowling attack as, just occasionally, they were both available. On the subject of matches in pocket it can be a dangerous oversight. My friend was playing one of his first league games and batted number eleven after tea. A gnarled, seasoned professional had ground his way to thirty odd, running between the wickets with loose change rattling in one pocket and a box of matches in the other. A delivery struck him on the pocket containing the matches and ignited them. The batsman tried to beat the flames with his cap and a black mark developed on his flannels.

The back garden season ran side by side with the cricket calendar. In winter, it was time for rugby and football. I devised a game based on the various rugby kicks and competitions between different countries. This was probably more of a pain for the neighbours than the cricket. With flat feet, my soft, round ball frequently went off at unpredictable angles. Football would likely be played with a mate. Looking back, it seems foolish to play penalties with the goalkeeper defending a window. One Sunday afternoon, as Bobby Charlton, I slotted a spot kick into the top left corner. The lounge window caved in spectacularly with shards of glass covering the tea table set for my granny and grandad's visit.

# 5  Wickets down the Snicket

My back yard cricket kept me occupied for hours but was nothing compared to the quality of cricket available outside the back gate. When friends were available, we would set up on the narrow road which ran along the length of High Hill Grove. It was accessible to cars but back in the early sixties it was quiet most of the time. For me and my mates the bumps and cracks made for a teasing and testing cricket strip. On the off side was the red brick wall at the back of Ellis's Garage whilst on the leg side were our back gardens, all too close for comfort. A simple rule applied. Hit the ball in there and it was six and out. The offending batsman was always the one who had to retrieve it. He would gingerly opened the gate and virtually tip-toe to the ball before retiring at speed. Only occasionally was there any trouble. That could be when a neighbour came under fire from a stray six over midwicket whilst pegging out the washing or when their flowers were damaged. I'm sure that my square leg and mid-wicket drives were perfected on the back street of High Hill Grove, where you only stayed in if you kept the ball down.

The wicket was an oil drum. We clambered over into the garage's mucky rubbish tip, seeking out one of suitable size. No one seemed to mind or complain. Once the 'wicket' was in place, early morning, it would only be moved as cars came along. Otherwise, we batted, bowled and fielded for hours, well past the time when umpires would have called bad light and led the players off.

A second pitch existed in the car park of North Ribblesdale Rugby Club, just across the road at the front of the houses. This was trickier because it was private property and we took the risk of the secretary turning up in his car and giving us a right telling off. It was a wider area for fielding but from extra cover to third man the slope ran down awkwardly and brambles and nettles made for an uncomfortable experience chasing a ball. Grazed skin was common. We often took time out to sniff the empty beer barrels down the side of the club house, my first introduction to alcohol.

The extra space at the rugby club gave me chance to practise my John Price impression. When you play games of cricket for hours at a time, it is very easy to morph into one of your heroes with actions learned from black and white games on television. All the mannerisms and peculiarities of the cricketer had to be included. JSE Price played for Middlesex and England between 1961 and 1975. The one thing I remember about him was an exceptionally long run-up with an angled approach to the wicket. Try this on the back street and you'd have to start from a neighbour's kitchen. Wes Hall posed different problems. His long, straight run to the wicket could not happen at the rugby club. Well, not without demolishing the scout hut. It was easier on the back road where you could start in the middle distance. John Snow was a favourite of mine. Like Hall his run-up was straight. Snow was tall and lithe in the approach, with a hint of menace. I genuinely wished I was right-handed so that I could get make these impressions more genuine.

Another favourite of mine was Mushtaq Mohammed. I was the best left-handed Mushtaq Mohammed impersonator in our neighbourhood. The ball twirled from hand to hand as I ran in to the wicket at an angle, bowling flippers, wrong 'uns and leg breaks.

First in to bat, there was no other choice but Geoff Boycott. Then I could set my stall out for the morning. I would bat left-handed whilst mimicking John Edrich's upright, compact stance as he waited at the crease or Brian Close's pronounced bend of the body in stance with posterior sticking out, practised in the back garden. Wicketkeeping-wise I perfected every movement and nuance of Middlesex and England's John Murray. He was a stylish keeper who went through the same ritual before every delivery. He would always make contact with his cap

12

and his gloves would be touched together and jammed into place. Everything was done with grace. As for the fielder, well look no further than Colin Bland. Fielding was always the activity that I least liked in our childhood games. To me it was the poor relation behind batting, bowling and keeping but it helped when I became Colin Bland, swooping like an eagle in the covers and producing an almighty clang from the oil can as the throw with the flat delivery and trajectory was just too much for the batsman.

Here's a thirteen man squad of cricketers I was most likely to impersonate:

Geoffrey Boycott (Yorkshire), John Edrich (Surrey), Ken Barrington (Surrey), Brian Close (Yorkshire), Colin Bland (South Africa), Mushtaq Mohammed (Northants & Pakistan), Don Wilson (Yorkshire), John Snow (Sussex), Fred Trueman (Yorkshire), Ken Higgs (Lancashire), John Murray (Middlesex), Graham Mackenzie (Leicestershire & Australia), John Price (Middlesex)

There are many reasons why street cricket doesn't happen anymore. Imagine if it did. Our youngsters would likely be copying the styles of Josh Buttler, Jonny Bairstow or Jason Roy with reverse sweeps. Perhaps an audacious hit for six over the wicketkeeper's head would have been attempted. We wouldn't have contemplated that in my day. It would have put the vehicles in Ellis's car park under threat.

# 6  Settle Cricket Club

A significant part of my childhood was spent at Settle Cricket Club. It was a natural progression from the garden and artificial pitches in High Hill Grove. The Marshfield ground was overlooked by the limestone crags above the town and, unusually, had two levels, separated by a steep slope. My mates and I used to roll down it during the tea interval when we weren't knocking back bottles of Vimto and Dandelion and Burdock from the refreshment room on the top level, in the shadow of a giant sycamore tree. There were also packets of crisps with those blue bags of salt in them.

Marshfield became a second home in the summer months. I would take in the match day atmosphere at weekends and play on the outfield during the week with my mates. Settle ran teams in the Ribblesdale League. Geographically, the town was detached from the rest of the league teams which were on or over the border into Lancashire. There were twelve teams and matches against the likes of Clitheroe, Great Harwood and Whalley, part of a fixture list that had a familiar look season on season. None of those three were in the 2018 Division One. Only five remain in a nine-team league. This shows how changes in recent years have affected that status quo which I knew so well.

As well as the consistency of opponents there was also a reassuring stability about the Settle team sheet. I can still recite it now. These guys had ordinary lives and ordinary jobs but on Saturdays they became gods to me. Eric Mitchell, no relation, lived down my street and I was friends with his children. Eric batted number three, a left-hander who accumulated thousands of runs using a pair of ageing gloves that had a thumb protection on the end of a strip of elastic. He had to wind it round his wrist several times before sliding it into place. Eric carved many a big innings alongside Brian Horn and the dashing 'Chippy' Andrews. Colin Smith was a PE teacher and stylish number four. In later years, Mum and Dad moved on to the same avenue as Colin and I was still in awe of him, trying to catch a furtive glimpse as I went past. I stood near all-rounder Ken Foster at the 'Tour de Yorkshire' cycle race in Settle a couple of years back. As I cast brief glances towards him, my mind raced back to Marshfield, recalling vital innings scored at a good rate and medium-paced bowling with a lovely action. Mac Davidson, alias 'Rockbox' was a canny bowler and competitor. His son, Andrew, and a seemingly endless stream of grandsons have graced the scene since. Our wicketkeeper was Brian Hemingway, not built for pace but mighty effective all the same. His brother delivered our newspapers.

My childhood heroes - Settle Cricket Club First Team with Colin Smith cleverly inserted!

I watched countless games as a child, often from inside the score box which backed on to Marshfield Road. Later, it was moved next to the pavilion which stood in the shadow of a railway viaduct. The bridge carried trains up and down the iconic Settle-Carlisle railway. The line ran alongside the ground so I could get some train numbers at the same time. The tale goes that a well-struck ball once landed in a carriage and travelled seventy-two miles north to Carlisle, making it the longest hit in history. That was a favourite story of Dad's.

There was no more exciting day at Settle Cricket Club than when the county came to town. From 1946 until well into the 1960s there was a pre-season match against Yorkshire, the dominant team in the country. One of their heroes was local lad, Don Wilson. Wilson's dad was an ambulance superintendent who lived near the railway on the south side of town. It was just across from the bench that my mates and I spent hours on with Ian Allan compendiums waiting for trains to pass by. Wilson senior carved his son a rough bat from a piece of oak and Don spent hours hitting a tennis ball against the coal-house in the back yard. It was the Settle v Yorkshire game of 1953 that set the ball rolling for him. Like me some years later, he eagerly scanned the team list on the noticeboard outside Lamberts and discovered that he had been selected to play against the county. As usual, Yorkshire batted first and the time came for the fifteen year-old to bowl. The batsman was none other than the legendary Len Hutton. Hutton pushed the first two deliveries away before being bowled by the third. The ball went straight on and the great man missed it. It might not have been popular with the spectators but it was enough to gain Wilson an invitation to the Yorkshire nets the following spring. His batting failed to impress Arthur Mitchell, the Yorkshire coach. Facing Fred Trueman, the young lad missed time and again. Mitchell shouted down the net, 'What does tha' do for a livin?' Wilson was an apprentice joiner by trade. Back came the riposte, 'Well I suggest tha' fetch some bloody timber and board that end up!' Thankfully, the bowling side came out better. Yorkshire and England honours followed. Wilson was to play his part in the annual fixture over the following years, both on and off the pitch. Along with Phil Sharpe and others he was keen on light opera and took centre stage in many a post-match sing-song.

The crowds turn out for Settle's annual game against Yorkshire
(from the Eric Mitchell collection)

Yorkshire treated the Settle game as part of serious preparation for their county season and, as such, brought a strong team. Autographs were happily dispensed by our heroes. I ticked them off one by one. Ray Illingworth, Brian Close, Doug Padgett, Phil Sharpe... There was one that eluded me, a notable exception. Fred Trueman did not give his easily. I eventually got it by giving my autograph book to Eric Mitchell and he asked for me at the post-match evening do. Occasionally, guests appeared. My autograph book shows Ken Barrington and Bernard Constable, both Surrey players. There was also Middlesex and England's Fred Titmus. I will never forget Yorkshire's John Hampshire striking a ball majestically over mid-off through the bedroom window of one of the houses that overlooked the ground on Marshfield Road. The occupant was clearly not a cricket fan and came out creating blue murder.

Yorkshire's Vic Wilson heads back into the Settle Pavilion
(from the Eric Mitchell collection)

Yorkshire cricketers were part of folklore in the Broad Acres. As with the Settle team, their team list is forever imprinted on my brain. Boycott, Taylor, Padgett, Sharpe, Hampshire, Close, Illingworth, Hutton, Binks, Trueman, Wilson, Nicholson. Pick eleven from that twelve and they would give England a run for their money. In the days when winning the County Championship meant something it was as talented a county side as there has ever been.

# 7 'Tally-wagging'

I did a lot of 'tally-wagging' at the Marshfield ground in Settle. This involved keeping the scorebox up to date. I haven't been back since it became electronic but doubt that working it now would be as much fun as back in the sixties. The two official scorers, one from each team, would sit at a rudimentary wooden surface looking out across the playing surface over their large-size scorebooks. In the days before multi-coloured pens, their preferred tool was usually a sharpened pencil, with a rubber handy. Several of us would work round them, avoiding distractions but needing to check on details when necessary. Replacing one number with another was all fairly straightforward. The only slightly complicated part was advancing the team total, a process which involved an arrangement of oily chains and cogs. Our vantage point was up a short ladder. We peered through a space which could only be filled if a batsman scored a century. I loved it. There was a sense of satisfaction and a hint of power as I looked across the ground through my bolt hole. All those out there, players, umpires and spectators alike, would look many times in our direction as the game wore on. Not yet ready to play for my club, I nevertheless felt at the heart of the action. We even got a free tea! Occasionally, I would hop out to help find a ball that had gone into the long grass on the railway embankment below the Settle-Carlisle line or climb eagerly on to the back of a bench to look over the whitewashed wall next to us, first on the scene to survey any damage in the adjoining back gardens by a ball struck high and hard for six.

Picture across Marshfield showing the old scoreboard (from the Eric Mitchell collection)

Scoring became rather less formal for the midweek Medal competition. This involved evening games of twenty overs each. There would be local groups, such as pubs and firms. They went under a range of interesting and amusing names. The idea re-emerged half a century later as T20 cricket, becoming the fastest growing form of the game and a financial saviour. Modern players dressed in coloured outfits can now make a fortune. There is background music, fireworks and razzmatazz aplenty. Back in the sixties I could foresee none of this as I watched Saturday team players pitching in alongside the butcher, the baker and the candlestick maker. This was the annual opportunity for anyone and everyone to appear at the home of Settle Cricket Club. Players of all shapes and sizes turned up, most with very few aspirations of greatness but keen to have a laugh followed by a few drinks at the Golden Lion or the Talbot. There was no restriction on clothing. Shirts flapped loose and tight-fitting trousers caused embarrassment when bending over. Attempts to put pads on could be comical, particularly after a quick fall of wickets. It was not unusual to see an incoming batsman trotting towards the wicket in a clumsy way wearing just one pad, flapping around his leg.

Each player could bowl a maximum of two overs while batsmen had to retire at 30. It sounds informal but my goodness it could be competitive. Hard fought encounters provided ripe entertainment for the regulars who sat shoulder to shoulder barracking from start to finish. They loved it. It was their best entertainment of the week.

To avoid any unfair domination, no side could field more than four regular cricketers but it didn't stop a 'ringer' or two being included. They would be the ones who nobody else recognised but were good enough to reach 29 deliberately before hitting a four or six. It was all a welcome change from the Saturday league encounters and made for a quite different scorebox experience. Frequent shouts of 'NAME?' would be called out when there was a bowling change or catch taken. If a reply wasn't forthcoming, an alternative would be entered in the book. It might be 'Black Trousers', 'Blue Shirt' or some such description to identify the mystery player.

I watched on avidly as a child and eventually the day came when I could play my own small part. It was 1973, my last summer at school. My school team had been included in the Medal competition that year but having been unable to play in the first round defeat I immediately qualified for another side. I was picked up by Peter Roberts who had organised teams for years. We won the competition and a small trophy still sits in my study, slightly battered and missing its support but a proud reminder of an early triumph in my cricketing career. It was my first-ever cricketing reward.

My first cricket trophy, Settle medal competition 1973

Settle Cricket Club gave me a good grounding in a game that was to give me much pleasure. I was to play and watch a lot more around Yorkshire over the coming years. After hours and hours spent playing on the boundary, scoring from the box, looking for lost balls and watching the action at Marshfield, my apprenticeship had been served. All that remained was to play league cricket for my home town club. More of that later.

# 8  School Cricket

In 'The Train Journey' we found comedian Tony Hancock in London faced with a very long journey north to a theatrical engagement in Giggleswick. Bear with me if you are under sixty. Despite Hancock referring to the village as 'the cultural centre of the north' it took a lot to convince the ticket officer that Giggleswick actually existed but an encyclopedic knowledge of the area from Sid James and a leaf through the timetable manual produced a result, 'Change at Leeds'.

Well, Giggleswick has very much existed for me. It's a mile or two down the road from Wigglesworth, uncomfortably close to the Lancashire border. My cricket-loving father-in-law used to wind me up by claiming I wasn't true Yorkshire as our water came from Stocks Reservoir just on the Red Rose side.

The school bearing the same name as the village formed an important part of my cricketing education as well as my academic in the days before I started paying adult match fees in league cricket. The team pictures from 1967 onwards show a portly figure with an uncool fringed hairstyle compared to some of the others in the group. Arms were always folded on the front row, behind the back if standing. A serious expression showed a reluctance to smile. I didn't have the most photogenic set of gnashers. The tell-tale line around each leg indicated that there was room to unpick the material and make them longer as I grew. My boots, pasted with whitener, always looked as if they were held together by tape.

It's funny how cricketing achievements stand out more clearly in my mind than results in class. Thirty-five wickets in my last year, swinging the final ball of the House final over square leg for six and victory. I came away from

Giggleswick with a modest understanding of Latin, the ability to play Fives and a variety of ties. There was a tie for everything. More importantly I had a platform to push forward with my cricket career. I played a lot of cricket at school in the late sixties and early seventies.

Giggleswick and Settle are separated by the River Ribble and I had crossed it one wintry day to do my Eleven-plus examination at Settle High School (which was in Giggleswick). Mum and Dad were concerned because I had tonsillitis but I figured there was only one chance. It didn't hold me back and I did enough on the various tests to get a place at Catteral Hall. This was the junior school of Giggleswick, a public school far posher than anything I'd met in my short life. Fortunately, my fees were paid for thanks to a generous endowment from an Old Boy. There's no way my parents could have afforded otherwise. It was September 1965 when I walked up the drive towards Catteral Hall, dressed in my new school uniform, shorts and striped black and red cap. This was a totally new world for me and, fortunately, a few of my class mates had also gained places. Day pupils were in the minority. This was a boarding school. There were quaint traditions and everyone seemed to have a quirky nickname. Days became longer as I was introduced to a wide range of extra-curricular activities. The model railway club was a favourite of mine. I read books like '1066 and All That' and Jennings. Sport was big and after a diet of football and rugby, cricket came along in term three.

The main pitch was next to the main A65 road to Kendal and access was down a magnificent line of trees called Chestnut Walk, on account of the fact that they were chestnuts. Alongside the field was a rifle range used by the Senior School and it was every junior boy's dream to swing a shot over square leg, clearing the building and landing in the rough ground on the far side. A short ball from the Chestnut Walk end and the eyes lit up. A pronounced swing of the bat was followed by either a glorious feeling as the ball sailed over the range or that most disheartening of sounds as leather met timber and the wicket tumbled behind you. It was always worth a dart, holding play up for a short while but gaining respect among your peers. I managed it a few times.

My mind went back to Mr. Plumridge and his games lessons on Bond Lane field. I was determined not to let him down. Circular pegs bearing our names would be positioned in holes on the main board while we were reading quietly after lunch. I had become used to this during the winter months. Sometimes I could see the selection committee through the glass partition in the door. The Headmaster, pipe in mouth, and the games teacher pondered over who to put where. Any one of the wooden pegs in their hands could bear my name. This merely served to whip up my enthusiasm and nerves. It mattered to me where I was placed. On the bell, the games shy walked slowly to discover their fate during the long afternoon ahead while the sport needy raced across to the boards.

Catteral Hall had plenty of equipment and access to cut strips for wickets. This was a new world for me. We also had proper practice nets and I remember standing near them one day talking to the Headmaster and cricket master about being naturally left-handed. They wanted to develop me as a slow left arm bowler to add variety. It was nice to feel wanted. I made it into the school team. Teams needed proper kit so a pair of flannels was bought for me by Mum and Dad. I played well enough to be made captain and get my colours, a white peaked cap with the school initials on the front. I needed the largest size. I still have it. It doesn't fit any more. Not by a long way.

It all became very civilised with away trips to Prep Schools such as Grosvenor House, Malsis and Aysgarth. There would be handshakes all round, polite applause when appropriate and proper cricket teas comprising sandwiches and cakes. As captain I was expected to be an example to others on and off the pitch. Matches were well-attended by parents who invariably brought treats for sons if boarders. Some knew what they were talking about, most didn't and spent much of the time gossiping. These were the ones who bought their offspring brand new bats which were way too big, 'so they could grow into them.'

Catteral Hall captain 1967, age 13. I wasn't built for speed.

At age thirteen we all moved on to 'Big School' and I worked my way up the various age group teams. The Colts, or Under 15s, were run by Mr. Dean, aka Gabber. Gabber Dean was a good coach but operated in his own time scale which was invariably ten minutes later than everyone else. As captain I was caught between coach and team. My friend from primary school, 'Pinky' Newhouse, had bypassed this level by now and gone straight to play for the first team. He was a leg spinner who could turn the ball prodigiously. I was somewhat jealous of his promotion, no, I was proper jealous but got on with it and bizarrely played one of my best innings after drinking a can of Whitbread in the pavilion. Goodness knows how it got there. Sadly, my parents are no longer with us but it does mean that I can 'come out' about my crafty slurp.

Eventually, I joined 'Pinky' in the first team in 1972, the season after coping with Gabber's ways. Having made my way round the various out-grounds on the school playing fields I was now on hallowed turf. Top Pitch remains one of my favourite grounds.

Top Pitch from above

It was in the shadow of the school Chapel with superb views across Giggleswick and Settle to the limestone scars beyond. There was quite a climb to get there but it was worth the effort. Around the pavilion walls were wooden boards on which were painted the names of previous teams. Players in red, captain in gold. I couldn't wait to see my name added to the roll of honour after the first season.

There was a new first team coach. John Mayall was not the blues musician but more prosaically my English teacher. Anyway, he made me team secretary. I wasn't really sure what it meant but it sounded important and presumably guaranteed me a place in the team. The following year I was made captain. Red letters turned to gold on the pavilion wall! There was a good squad of players with several who had come through with me from primary school days in Settle and would have enjoyed early sessions with Jim Plumridge. My first season as captain was unexpectedly followed by a second in 1973 when I flunked my 'A' levels, forcing an extra year at school. No one did gap years back then. I felt sorry for 'Pinky' who would have had his chance otherwise but that's how it is in the cut-throat world of school sport. We lost only two out of fifteen games which was very respectable for a smaller school like ours. Mum and Dad walked up the hill to watch over the wall behind the bowler's arm and I like to think that their effort was not in vain. It was a very good way to end my time in schools cricket. I wasn't a finely-honed athlete with a six pack. My boots were still as tatty as those I first wore and my flannels still fastened tight round my midriff but it had been a wonderful eight summers.

First Team pavilion at Giggleswick School, near where Mum and Dad came to watch me play

# 9  Cricket Festivals

The final swansong was the festival. Festivals were the traditional end of year events and they involved the same four schools - St Bees, Durham, Woodhouse Grove and Giggleswick. Each school played the other three on successive days and between matches the aim was to have as much fun as possible. I scraped in at the end of my Colts year and then, with three years in the first team, it meant that I was part of all four schools home festivals. St Bees came first for me. Up on the Cumbrian coast, it was the kind of place where residents turned out to watch the lights change. I was the youngest in the party. I hadn't even played for the first team yet. Demob happy at the end of their school life, the leavers headed off in search of alcohol. I tagged along as my teammates earmarked the village pub on the first night. I don't mind admitting that I was nervous. I reflected on the fact that this would be only my third contact with alcohol. I had only previously smelt the dregs around the barrels at the rugby club and had the can of Whitbread in the Colts pavilion. I ordered a half of Tartan, worried that I might throw up in front of my team mates as soon as I had taken a mouthful. I stayed on it for the rest of the night, the one glass that is, not Tartan.  I woke up next morning with a pair of socks stuck in my mouth. Apparently, someone didn't like my snoring. There were footprints across the ceiling above my head but they didn't look my size. To this day I have no idea how they got there.

My last Festival was on home soil. I was more of a social animal by then and looked across at the youngest member of the party, no doubt experiencing the same nerves that I had three years earlier. A period of extremely sunny and warm weather had produced firm, dry conditions. The home soil was very compacted. With our good side there was every chance we could do well. Dougie Vincent had other ideas. Dougie was a decent lad who we knew from previous years, winter and summer. He went to Woodhouse Grove, between Leeds and Bradford. It has always had good cricketing pedigree. Graham Roope coached cricket there for many years and former pupils such as Ajmal Shahzad and Kathryn Leng have gone on to make a mark in the game.

Fielding on Top Pitch

The 1973 Festival at Giggleswick was Dougie Vincent's finest hour. I lost touch with him but doubt he has achieved anything comparable since. He clobbered 381 runs in three games for once out. Giggleswick got hammered to the tune of 200 not out in a total of 275 for 6. There were six sixes and twenty-three fours. I've never seen an innings like it. The road over High Rigg, Mum and Dad's viewpoint, was peppered as shot after shot went into orbit. It was a sobering experience, unlike the night before. My mate John Robinson got redder and redder as he covered from square-leg to long-on in stifling weather. We girded our loins at tea and somehow survived, reaching 184 for

8, but it had been an amazing display of power hitting and a dramatic way to finally end my time at school.

# 10 The games people play

Picture the scene. It is the peace and quiet of a campsite near Pitlochry in Scotland. It is a late sixties August and the Mitchell family are pitched up in a dormobile. It is the first and last time that we have had such a holiday. Dad would be writing notes on what has happened during the day, Mum would be tidying as she always did and sister Janet likely reading a magazine. The quiet would be interrupted by a distinctive soundtrack. It is the sound made when a hexagonal metal roller is propelled along a hard table top. I am sitting at the table, yet again immersed in the world of 'Owzthat'. It is one of the two great cricket games of my childhood. The other was 'Discbat'.

'Owzthat' still exists. Two rollers make up the set and that is all, apart from the blue tin that holds them between matches. The game is small enough to fit in your pocket but big enough to take over your life.

Owzthat. Small in size but big in my life.

It was in my top three of treasured possessions, up there alongside my bike and my cricket bat. There was a cheaper alternative where you carved six notches in the end of a pencil and rolled it. You could get away with that in the classroom if you needed your fix but there was nothing like the iconic rollers. They were the real deal. The smaller one was labelled 1,2,3,4,6 and OWZTHAT. With this, you totted up the runs for each batsman, until the OWZTHAT showed up and then the second roller came into play. This one had, 'Bowled', 'Stumped', 'Caught', 'Not Out', 'No Ball' and 'LBW'. There was a one in three chance of surviving the appeal.

'Owzthat' was taking over our imaginary sporting worlds fifty years before 'FIFA' came along. Entire Test series evolved in front of my eyes. I was chairman of selectors, manager and chief coach as my teams toured the world. Compiling fantasy teams has always been one of the great delights of cricket. I spent many a happy hour selecting teams. The 'B's' might face the 'S's:

Geoff Boycott, Bob Barber, Peter Burge, Ken Barrington, Basil Butcher, Eddie Barlow, Keith Boyce, Trevor Bailey, Jimmy Binks, Richie Benaud, Bishen Bedi

Phil Sharpe, Rt. Rev. David Sheppard, Ken Suttle, David Steele, MJK Smith, Garry Sobers, John Shepherd, Jack Simmons, John Snow, Ken Shuttleworth, Derek Shackleton.

Every scoring shot and dismissal was dutifully recorded in a proper book. Averages would be worked out meticulously. Reality and fantasy could sit alongside each other in my scorebooks. For every game that I followed live, there must have been at least fifty fictional encounters with my two rollers. You wouldn't believe how much fun could be had from that pair. It quickly became obsessive. I mention Pitlochry because that was when playing the game dominated my whole week in Scotland. I had to get back from the park or the town to start the next game, I rushed meals down. I needed my fix. If you see my sister, mention it but stand back when you do.

The most surprising thing about the success of 'OWZTHAT' is that it was clearly based on luck. A batsman had an equal chance of scoring a 1 or a 6. The rollers did not contain computer chips holding information on players' previous form. Despite a career batting average of 11.75, Yorkshire's Tony Nicholson once scored 121, 153 and 118 for me in a three-Test series.

You willed your favourites to score big but the rollers did not respect reputations. They would catch on a snag in the carpet or tip over the edge of a table and up would pop 'OWZTHAT'. You just knew that if you had rolled a perfect one, it wouldn't have happened that way. However, you couldn't re-roll it. That would be cheating and the thin end of the wedge. I know exactly where to find mine, even to this day, and it wouldn't take much for me to start rolling again.

Discbat was equally obsessive. Here, two players faced each other across a table on which was a green cloth representing the playing area. The bowler had a ball bearing and a chute to propel it in the direction of the batsman whose 'bat' was a circular metal shape attached to a length of string which hung down from a metal structure. The bat could be swung back and forth, aiming to strike the ball as it headed down the cloth. Over-exuberance occasionally caused the structure to collapse and repairs were needed. Oval white lines across the cloth marked the number of runs scored with boundaries for hitting the edge. Fielders were placed strategically, hoping for a catch as the ball nestled in a pouch on their base.

The opportunities were endless and a small group of us formed our own Test teams. We devised series home and away and sought ways of outdoing our opponents. The ball bearing could be pelted at speed or made to perform all manner of tricks when delivered slowly, early equivalents of the doosra.

I based my team on authors and gave it the title Buck Isle. Our team colours were light blue. We faced the might of Plunket, Fotheringay and Capel Isle. My players' names came off the shelves and were reborn as cricketers. My cricketers. I loved the Jennings books so Anthony Buckeridge was an early choice. He batted number four. I saw him as an accumulator, the cornerstone of the line-up. He had a wife and three children and was in every way a solid, reliable sort. Another favourite book, '1066 and All That', produced Sellar and Yeatman. Yeatman was a tall, rangy medium-paced bowler. Sellar was an all-rounder, medium-paced like his close friend Yeatman and capable of scoring quickly in the lower order. Cathcart-Borer was my classically educated number three. Controversially, he was a 'she' in reality, Mary by name, so a pretty interesting back story could be compiled there. WJ Riley, an all-rounder of immense value to the team, was eventually joined by his two brothers.

And so, my imaginary cricketers fought my battles. They developed characters, strengths and weaknesses. Some were retired, others came in. There was a ready-made assembly line of young talent coming off my bookshelves. They all became part of Buck Isle folklore through much of my teenage years.

Reading back over this section makes me look like a proper nerd.

# 11 My admiration for Sir Geoffrey

Cricketers by-and-large are uncontroversial beings but within their ranks lie those who have always divided opinion. Geoffrey Boycott was certainly one of those. Ian Chappell and Kevin Pieterson are in the same club. As a player, a person and a commentator Boycott has triggered as many arguments as the runs he has amassed over a long and distinguished career. There is a large area of empty middle ground between those who admire him with a passion and detest him with fervour. I suppose that is the nature of the beast with these gritty, uncompromising types. I have rows of Yorkshire books in my study from the sixties and seventies. Dad got them as editor of the 'Dalesman' magazine and passed them on after he had done a short review. He never fully read them. Occasionally, I got to review one or two for him. I can testify to the amount of space devoted to the disruptive part that Geoffrey Boycott played at Headingley. Despite all that, he was my cricketing hero.

I cannot remember a moment when I became a Boycott fan but he was the first name that I looked for in the daily and evening newspapers. It wasn't about fast scoring and spectacular boundaries, more the steady accumulation of runs and solidity at the top of the order. I was a shy youngster with few frills. I rarely strayed from the straight and narrow because I hated getting into trouble. I wasn't the sort to ring a doorbell and run off or pinch a toy from off the shelves at Lamberts. In Boycott's straight bat defence and impenetrable technique I saw someone who I could relate to.

With characteristic strokes such as the on-drive and the back foot shot through the covers Boycott amassed over eight thousand Test runs at 47.72 and nearly fifty thousand first-class runs at 56.83. He denied himself thirty Test opportunities in his prime, between 1974 and 1977, and would, surely, have been the first Englishman to 10000 runs. He returned against Australia in 1977 and sparked yet another controversy as he ran out local hero Derek Randall in the Third Test at Trent Bridge. Boycott was wise to stay out in the middle and compile a century. The Fourth Test was at Headingley. Just five days earlier, Boycott had scored his ninety-ninth career century, for Yorkshire against Warwickshire. None of the previous century of centuries club had reached this landmark in a Test Match, let alone on their home ground. England batted. I went without food on the packed Western Terrace, so nervous was I about the possibility of witnessing a piece of cricketing history from my hero. Beside me, my wife-to-be knitted on contentedly. There was a brief scare as Boycott was dropped by Rodney Marsh on 22. He reached 36 by lunch, 79 at tea. This was typically steady accumulation. The Aussies upped-the-ante and tried to unsettle him. An arm ball from Ray Bright brushed thigh or bat through to Marsh. Even some of Boycott's team-mates thought he was caught and next batsman, Graham Roope, was out of his seat and putting his gloves on so convinced was he. As it was, Roope was to be there when the century was reached, just before six o'clock. He jumped out of the way as an on-drive, appropriately, raced to the fence at the Football Ground end. We rose en masse. I'm sure a stitch or two was dropped in the excitement. Forty years on, Boycott was in the 'Test Match Special' box when Jonathan Agnew tricked him with a memorable wind-up, claiming that the statistics from the England v Rest of the World series in 1970 were to be downgraded from first-class status. This meant that the Headingley century was Boycott's 99th. Boycott took it in remarkably good spirit. It was a classic TMS moment.

So there we are, steady, obdurate, an accumulator of runs throughout his career…with one notable exception. It will always stand out in the minds of those who go back that far. The scene was the traditional end of season highlight, the final of the Gillette Cup. This was the mother of all cricket knockout competitions. Yorkshire played Surrey on September 4th 1965. It was a dead pitch and a slow outfield. There had been rain leading up to the game. Yorkshire batted first and made 317, the highest ever total in the competition. The 24 year-old Boycott played with a freedom and dominance that belied his later reputation. It was commanding strokeplay and he made 146 runs.

In recent years, Boycott has battled cancer as stubbornly as he had held the world's finest bowlers at bay. He emerged as an honest and authoritative commentator who still has much to give the game. Now, as I write, he is recovering from heart surgery. The grit and determination forged on the cricket fields in the mining towns of the West Riding brought him through.

I was so absorbed by my favourite cricketer that in later years I painted him in oils. From a picture, not live. Rod Marsh was behind the stumps. I often thought whether to take it to a match and try to get the great man to sign it for me but I didn't want to spoil anything and come away feeling disappointed.

My painting of Sir Geoffrey

# 12 The Pink

Saturday was the day of the Sporting Pink. Anyone under a certain age won't have a clue what that means. Others will remember it as a distinctive newspaper devoted to sport and produced on pink paper. Sadly, the Pink has now gone, deemed surplus to requirements in our modern world. Back in the sixties the Pink reached Settle around six o'clock on a Saturday evening, winter and summer. In the days before information at the press of a button, this paper was the 'bees-knees' with scores and updates aplenty on the day's action, particularly on the outside pages. Inside would be more reflective pieces prepared during the week. This was one newspaper I didn't need to share with my family.

Through the week, the Telegraph and Argus kept me in touch with the cricket. I would race down the snicket to the newsagents around tea time, waiting for the delivery from Bradford. The bundle of papers was dropped off the 'Pennine' bus at around five twenty and I was invariably there as it hit the pavement outside Speight and Watson's with a dull 'thud'. The string was cut open, a pristine copy would be taken off the top of the pile and handed to me. No money was needed. It went on the bill. Before it got into family hands, I could spend the short walk back down t' snicket checking up on the Yorkshire score. By then it would be three hours or so behind the times but there was always the 'stop press' to fall back on, a strip of blank page in which the editor would put updates. A brief summary would suffice. Runs, wickets, and main scorers. It might read Yorkshire 154-2 (Boycott 73 no, Hampshire 27 no). All was well with the world when I saw that Yorkshire had made a good start and that my hero was among the runs yet again. The walk home might then turn into a skip or a run, taking care to dodge the pavement stones with cracks in them. 'Step on a crack and you break your back.'

The 'Argus' still exists. It's in tabloid form now. Sadly, I don't see the Pink any more, or its green relative from other newspapers. Nowadays I find updates on my mobile in an instant but, believe me, it's not as exciting as scouring the Sporting Pink. Sometimes, I still find myself thinking about it on a Saturday evening.

# 13  College Cricket

Having not strayed more than a mile or two from home so far, it was off to college in 1973. I was heading for the City of Leeds and Carnegie College, just down a terraced road or two from Headingley cricket ground. I was going to learn to be a teacher having turned my back on a career in journalism. Dad had taken me through the snow to Preston's Harris College for interview. I got a place on their journalism course but decided that I would have to wait awhile to write on cricket for the 'Daily Telegraph'. No, teaching was the obvious choice for me. It was a steady career with a reliable income, long holidays and an endless supply of pencils. I was to be made redundant twice.

For many students, the excitement of college came from the potential for a social explosion away from prying parents. It says a lot about me at that point in time, age 19, that I got more excited by the cricket ground in the middle of the college buildings. It had a pronounced slope and was surrounded by the halls of residence, boys on one side, girls on the other. It was a short-cut for many a male and female as they criss-crossed from one hall to another, often late at night. On one occasion, our Hall Tutor came across from the girls side when the fire alarm went off. That set tongues wagging. I also know of no other cricket ground where mischievous students used to take everything from a study and set it up identically on the outfield while the occupant was off campus, complete with working bedside lamp. That happened to my mate Marshy, his downfall sealed when he played 'Annie's Song' by John Denver just one time too often.

It was not the best standard of ground but, nevertheless, not far to go for a game. Carnegie College had a strong sporting reputation. I'll always remember Marshy being asked early on by another fresher what standard of basketball he had played. He proudly replied, 'Captained Kent. And you?' 'Captained England.'

I had to wait awhile for the chance to show what I was worth as a cricketer. Before then there were two terms of winter sport, a bit of academic work, teaching practice and a whole lot of learning about life. I had safely negotiated the freshers week, more than can be said for Chris who finished up near the cricket ground naked and in a laundry basket and Geoff who was strapped to a statue in the city centre after attempting his version of 'Je t'aime' in drag. By the summer I was adept at beer games such as 'Bunnies' and 'Names Off' and could walk round the outside of my hall of residence without touching the ground.

Come the cricket and I had my own sort of 'Marshy Moment' because whatever I could put down experience-wise, others could trump it. I soon found that I was in the company of some fine cricketers and for these guys college cricket was very much a second string. Saturdays saw them return to clubs in the Yorkshire, Bradford and Central Lancashire Leagues. They were paid to play league cricket and would turn out for midweek games against other colleges. The college captain was Jim Carnegie, a larger-than-life fourth-year student with flowing blonde hair. I suppose if he'd been called Jim Loughborough he would have gone elsewhere. I was reliably informed that Jim used to hit sixes through open study windows one-handed. He was the Beefy Botham of Beckett Park.

I played for college with some success. The main competition was the British College National Knockout Cup. 'Pinky', from Giggleswick School days, was now at Bede College in Durham, as was future Lancashire player, Gehan Mendis. They won the competition in 1974, beating us in the final. They needed seventy from the last seven overs and got them in six. Oh dear.

# 14  League Cricket

League cricket has been the bedrock of our amateur game and, despite recent changes in structure, remains so. Now we have more pyramid structures than the Egyptians. League cricket is the stuff that stokes the fires in the belly. It is the form of the game that turns many a meek and mild individual into a ferocious competitor when that boundary line is crossed. A friend of mine was typical. By day he was a respected teacher, genial company and generous with his time. That's until he took his place on a cricket field. As a batsman, he liked to wind the opposition up in subtle ways. A favourite was to back up at the non-striker's end and deliberately stay outside his crease when the shot had been made. He goaded the fieldsman into having a shy at his end and attempting a run out. As the ball was released he would return to the crease and, often, bonus runs would come as the throw went wide with no one backing up in the field. Many of us, to be fair, have tried it but my friend considered himself to be an expert. His was an effective strategy until a game at Preston. A large West Indian called Marvin fielded the ball from a push into the covers. Its horizontal course from Marvin's hand was missile-like. All three stumps were splayed in different directions, leaving my friend out of his crease and looking back stunned. A few seconds later he started his sorry walk from the field of play. The chewing gum went many a metre off the bat and the order of arrival back at the pavilion was bat, gloves, friend.

Another trick was to raise the ball's seam by applying nail power. I have known team mates do this so effectively that when it was tossed to me it lacerated my hand. The psychological twists and turns of an afternoon's league cricket are constantly fascinating. Issues can boil over from one game into the next, one year into another. Cricketers might forget the most basic details in their domestic life but, trust me, they never forget what happened on the pitch.

There is always something to play for in a league season. One team that I captained finished with the Most Improved Trophy by rising from bottom to third bottom. It was based on the points relative to the total in the previous season. We triumphed by 0.68%. There was frequent debate about the merits of such an achievement. The strongest clubs always advocated a win or lose policy whereas those with more meagre resources clung on with more relish to a system involving winning draws and losing draws.

There's many an experienced league cricketer who has stuck with one team and maybe played on just fifteen or twenty grounds. My teaching career took me on a circular route round the north of England. I stopped off several times and must have notched up over a hundred grounds. League cricket always appealed to the competitive side of my nature. Trophies rarely came my way but that's not to say the experience wasn't pleasurable and challenging. I won't be remembered as one of the great players at any club I represented. Most of the time, I ended up between first and seconds. As at school I bowled slow left arm without spinning the ball a lot and it was my batting that developed more obviously. Greater success came in the second half of my career when I moved to opening the batting, a position that I enjoyed. I was a stronger leg side player. The drive through mid-wicket, nurtured on the back road in Settle, brought me a lot of runs but there was always the risk of an LBW.

I tasted league cricket for the first time in the early seventies when I turned out for Settle firsts and, occasionally, seconds in the Ribblesdale League. It just overlapped my schooldays. I couldn't wait for the team sheets to be posted on the board outside the newsagents, sandwiched between funeral details and items for sale. I pictured a group of men huddled round a table in the clubhouse, pints in front of them, discussing my merits. *'Should we give that young lad Mitchell another go? Mind you, we're a bit short of cars.'* If not selected my own personal inquest would last the rest of the day. Disappointment was always followed by a fierce determination to show 'em next time.

This was a quite different experience from the friendly, public school form of the game that I had been used to where sporting declarations were expected and fancy caps and blazers were de rigueur. It was a far tougher environment. Grudging respect was shown but no quarter given. Away matches were played across the border in Lancashire within sight of relics of the mills and factories of the Industrial Revolution. Every team had legendary figures who had been the backbone for years. Sons began to emerge to take their fathers' places, like Andrew Davidson at Settle. He played at the age of thirteen. Lancashire coach, Glen Chapple, played alongside his father, Mike, at Earby.

The professionals were key to success. It was a privilege to play alongside them but they had to earn their corn and captains gave them plenty of chance to do so. It was not unusual for the pro to bowl from one end throughout and this limited the opportunities for a young bowler like myself. There was never chance to bowl a long spell. I might get six or seven overs if lucky. I may be needed to break a partnership. Having done so, the strike bowlers would come back. I took three wickets a few times for the first team at Settle, never more. As a batsman I would likely come in trying to save a game or scoring quick runs at the end of the innings. That was the price you paid for first team action. The second team obviously offered more. My performances led to mentions in the 'Craven Herald' on a Friday. After taking 3 for 27 in seven overs in victory against Whalley in 1973 the paper reported that *'Dennis Mitchell helped Stanley (the pro) do the damage.'* Dennis Mitchell, that well-known spelling error. 'Dane' became a more common misprint. On other occasions I was simply mistaken for someone totally different. Whenever I got a duck, the paper never made a mistake. Settle was a good grounding in league cricket but after leaving home for college I was to play just a handful more games in 1977.

My next challenge was a tough one. Whilst at college in Leeds I played for Bradford Cricket Club. Their opening batsman, John Ridgeway, used to play at Settle and invited me along. It was at a time in the mid-seventies when Bradford left the Bradford League and joined the Yorkshire League. It was a move not without repercussions. Several first team regulars decided not to go with the rest. They wanted to stay local. An open door and a route to all the Yorkshire County out grounds beckoned for me. Bradford played at Park Avenue, the ground on which my grandad and I had watched the Australians all those years ago. It was still attached to the county club. Yorkshire played 307 first class games there between 1881 and 1996. Park Avenue had one of those features you wouldn't get today. On the other side of the stand opposite the pavilion was a professional football club. Bradford Park Avenue played in the Football League from 1908 to 1970. Its heyday was around the First World War. Ninth in the First Division in 1914-15 was as good as it got. As I arrived next door to play cricket, the football club had gone into liquidation and become members of the Bradford Amateur Sunday League.

Without a car and, more importantly, a driving licence, I got used to hopping on to a bus in Far Headingley and making the short journey 'next door' to Bradford for matches and midweek net practices. No need this time to go looking for team sheets on a noticeboard outside a newspaper shop. Postcards started arriving in my mail at college. They contained details of weekend games and times. There was quite a bit of travelling required, far more than in the locally-formed Bradford League. I quickly became familiar with the M62, ensuring three points of contact with the car as it sped along at 80 mph plus if the second team wicketkeeper was at the wheel. I started in the second team and did well enough to make the step up. Bradford had drafted in some former pros from Derbyshire and it was pretty serious stuff. Soon I was receiving details of some tasty cricket days-out. One by one I picked off the county grounds. There were more in those days, of course. Imagine my reaction to be reading details of the First Team game at Scarborough, *'Please meet at the Cricketers Arms opposite Scarborough CC, North Marine Road at 12:30 pm. Captain requires attendance at practice on Thursday next.'*

Six weeks later,

*'First Team v Leeds at Headingley, 2 pm. Please meet in Bradford club bar at 12:15 pm. Bring member's card owing to County game.'*

Scarborough was a wonderful experience and I was to go back a few years later with another club, but Headingley was the pinnacle. The lad from down the snicket had reached a prize wicket, a Test match venue and the home of the greatest county. There weren't many spectators around that day. Bradford batted first and, as I reached the square, I felt as if I was on an island in a huge flat green sea. To quote that commonly-used adjective, it was 'surreal'. The turf was different and the pavilion position had changed over the years but I was still walking in the footsteps of the greatest. The same patch of ground on which Bradman had scored two triple centuries back in the thirties, on which John Edrich scored 310 not out against New Zealand in 1965 was now, briefly, home for the afternoon. I remembered watching that Edrich innings on black and white television. And we still hadn't seen Sir Geoffrey's hundredth hundred in 1977 and the 'Botham' match in 1981. Perhaps thinking too much about the weight of history, I didn't last long with the bat but did better with the ball, including bowling a maiden over to Yorkshire's Jim Love, leaving extra cover with stinging, reddened palms as he stopped six sumptuous drives! My part in the game was peripheral but that didn't matter. I had been there, ticked it off and bowled a maiden.

There was definitely less room for error at this level. The first mistake with the bat was likely to be your downfall and a loose delivery was punished heavily. I still remember Scarborough's Tony Moor swinging me high over my head and into the football ground at Park Avenue. It was a relief to get back into the second team on occasions. There were some good lads and plenty of banter at that level. I felt comfortable ability-wise.

In August 1974, the first team played at Harrogate. Opening the bowling for Harrogate was one of Yorkshire's greatest, FS Trueman. 'Fiery' Fred was now just Fred. He was understandably past his best and after his first delivery needed running repairs on flannels which had burst open at the waist. He still had pace, even at the age of 43. I wasn't going to risk wearing one of my old Giggleswick School caps when I batted, knowing his famous disregard for such headwear and those who wore it. Harrogate had a useful side, including Peter Squires, the former British Lions winger. Squires was a decent cricketer and on Yorkshire's books at the time. As you can imagine, he ran a very quick single. There were also a couple of the schoolboy cricketers I had played against at Giggleswick. Peter Ingham and Peter Whiteley had both played for Ashville College in Harrogate. It was a school with close links to the county and they both went on to play for Yorkshire. My own aspirations had ended at a packed set of schoolboy nets at Headingley where it was difficult to make an impact among seventy or eighty others. The coaches pretty much knew their favoured players and one I remember was Graham Stevenson who was a cocky young man but talented as well. He was to play 177 games for Yorkshire between 1973 and 1986 and two Tests for England before dying all too soon in 2014, following a stroke at the age of 58. A week later I had a trial for Lancashire Federation, through the Ribblesdale League. I didn't get through that one either.

I remember Bradford most for the opportunities it gave me to play at a high club level on wonderful grounds. Before moving to my first teaching job I had a season at Ilkley in the Airedale-Wharfedale League. Ilkley is a lovely town unless you are trying to drive through it at a busy time. No, at any time. It lies on the River Wharfe twelve miles north of Bradford, has a spa heritage and Victorian architecture and is surrounded by beautiful countryside. Nearby is that world famous Yorkshire icon, Ilkley Moor, the subject of a folk song that is an unofficial Yorkshire anthem. There is no better place to overlook the valley than from the Cow and Calf Rocks.

Not being able to drive, I took public transport and was picked up in town by skipper and local legend, Mike Clegg, a man who would make the all-time team of characters that I have met in cricket. The only thing we had in common was that we bowled slow left arm. It was my first taste of Airedale-Wharfedale cricket and we visited some lovely grounds, as you would expect from such a beautiful part of Yorkshire. Otley, Burley-in-Wharfedale, Follifoot... I don't remember much about performances but there was one moment when I chased a ball to the boundary and coughed my guts up. I had taken to smoking cigars and that persuaded me to give up.

Ilkley was to be a brief drinks break in my life as a cricketer. By contrast, my next destination was to entertain me for ten seasons. I started a teaching job in Hull. Previously I had played twice in East Yorkshire. The first was for college, the second for Bradford against Hull in the Yorkshire League. After the college game we had one or two and, bizarrely, put a five-barred gate on the top of the minibus. It wasn't there when we arrived back in Leeds. The Bradford league game was at the Circle on Anlaby Road. It was another county ground to tick off. The Circle had hosted first class cricket since 1899 and witnessed some milestone moments. Maurice Leyland scored 263 for Yorkshire against Essex in 1936, Herbert Sutcliffe 234 against Leicestershire in 1939 and Basil D'Oliviera 227 for Worcestershire against Yorkshire in 1974. Johnny Wardle took nine wickets against Sussex in 1954. Among those taking eight were Wilfred Rhodes (v Hampshire, 1900), George Hirst (v Leicestershire, 1907) and Hedley Verity (v Leicestershire, 1939). That's a pretty impressive hall of fame.

Sadly, The Circle is no longer visible, having been demolished in 2001. The sporting accent has changed and the modern replacement, the KCOM Stadium, is home to both Hull City (football) and Hull FC (rugby league). Just across the railway line behind the stadium is the thirty acre site of the former Botanical Gardens. It is where my teaching career began in 1977. Hymers College was an all-boys Independent School, founded in 1887. I had taken a job in the Junior School, part of which involved running the cricket. My classroom looked across a stretch of land which contained no less than four cricket squares. My new boss, Norman Ransom, was a diehard Yorkshire fan. What could be better?

East Yorkshire had not been a fertile market for producing county cricketers but there was one in the great Yorkshire side of the 1960s. Wicketkeeper, Jimmy Binks, was a Hull boy. His father was a keen cricketer who played locally for the GPO and Hull $2^{nd}$ XI. His fingers were gnarled and misshapen as a result of standing up to the stumps for every bowler. For this reason, he wanted his son to be a bowler but Jimmy would have nothing of it. He wanted to be like his dad. Binks's career was to be unique. He was picked for every championship game played by Yorkshire between his debut in June 1955 and his retirement at the end of the 1969 season. That's 412 consecutive games. Unlike his father, Jimmy's hands were unmarked when he retired. As former Yorkshire cricketer, Ted Lester, said, 'He could have come straight off the field and played the piano.'

Hull Zingari Cricket Club was on Chanterlands Avenue, a couple of miles from my school. It had no connection with I Zingari, one of the oldest cricket clubs, other than the name which has an Italian source and means 'gypsies'. I knew Guy Williams who worked for Yorkshire TV in the area and was a member. He took me down. The sound of racket on ball reverberated from the squash courts as we walked through the Hull and East Riding Sports Club, of which Zingari was a part. At the far end of an otherwise empty bar was a thin figure with pint in hand and cigarette in mouth. Guy introduced me to my first Zingari stalwart, Derek Waite. Within a short time, I had joined. No money received, no contract, no sponsorship. All I had to do was pay to become a member. The first team played in the East Yorkshire Cup competition and the seconds in the Pennant Alliance, also in East Yorkshire. It was a large ground that used to be shared with rugby. The old stand still stood on the boundary edge. It was functional rather than beautiful. Houses bordered on three sides and tennis courts on the fourth.

Going in to bat at Hull Zingari

I played for the first team and captained the seconds. First team was a good standard under experienced skipper, Trevor Markham. I batted seven or eight and bowled when we needed a wicket. The part I really got involved in was the fielding. In my second season we won the East

Yorkshire Cup, the trophy for the league title. Time after time we kept runs down through tight and skilful bowling and reached the target with ease. Although I contributed relatively little with bat and ball, it was great to be part of a successful side. The away highlight was Scarborough where the pitches were always true and fast. The longest haul was cross-county up to Whitby, often on a Bank Holiday. Alastair Lyth was a fearsome foe. He hit a long ball, as did his son, Adam, who was to make his mark on the professional game for Yorkshire. My mate Richard played just once for the firsts. It was a Bank Holiday game at Whitby. He took the kit bag in his boot, didn't bat and didn't bowl.

Each ground and team had its own individualities. The Old Hymerians club was on the edge of town to the north and connected with the school that employed me. Bridlington played in Dukes Park and play might be held up as a train went slowly past, just leaving or entering Bridlington Station. Beverley was a favourite of mine, not far away which helped. I've never been one for long journeys. We always had tight tussles at Beverley. South Holderness played at Hedon and it was the home of Art Screeton. Art took a stack full of wickets each season, operating off a two pace run-up and without spinning a single ball. It was all in the flight and the psychology. Art was an unsettling presence at the other end. Those who hadn't faced him were transfixed by the shortest of 'runs' followed by the tantalising flight of the ball. Panic often set in. Batsman would advance down the pitch, to be caught, stumped or bowled at the hands of this most enigmatic of players. I visited Hedon in 2018. The memory of Art Screeton came straight back and a bead or two of sweat gathered on my brow.

My more memorable performances came for Zingari seconds, known as the An XI. I enjoyed opening the batting and scored half centuries a number of times. My career bowling peaked against Beverley Seconds at home on 6th May 1982. Troubled by a cross wind I had something like

0-32 off five overs and was close to taking myself off. I had one more over and finished with 8 for 48 off 12.4 overs! It was the second best analysis in the league that season.

Waiting to bat and digging the digger with daughter Helen

I always enjoyed playing Hornsea, the friendliest of clubs. There was Terry, a mild-mannered farmer off the pitch but reliable run accumulator on it. Pete was a tall, larger-than-life teacher. Helen, our eldest, started to arrive at a home game against Hornsea. Contractions were being timed in the clubhouse as we batted and by five the following morning she was with us. Nine months earlier, Susan and I had taken the Markham's son, Alastair, to watch England play New Zealand at Trent Bridge. It was day one and England scored 362 runs for seven wickets so you can imagine how entertaining the play was. The highlight was Ian Botham's 103 at a run a ball with fourteen fours and three sixes. Gower scored 62 and local favourite Randall 83. Then it was back to Trevor and Heather's for supper and a catch up of the video highlights on which the three of us could be spotted for a nano second. We were blurred, dark and in the background. There were clearer pictures from the first moon landing but we knew it was us. It was a wonderful day.

Whilst in Hull, I played cricket in the Newland Evening League. Zingari had a team but it was pretty much a closed shop so I looked elsewhere and found the British Transport Docks Board. Despite never setting foot inside the British Transport dock area, I was not alone. In fact, I can only remember one player qualifying for that reason. That was Hull Zingari first team regular, John Higo. There were some familiar faces connected with the Zingari club and we had a strong side. John Batty played Yorkshire League cricket for Hull, Mike Blackburn used to and Nigel Ling opened the batting for YPI across Chanterlands Avenue from the Zingari club. Nigel's playing for England Under 70s now. Other very competent cricketers would drift in and out. The clubs were closely situated within the city and games were played on Tuesday evenings. I had plenty of opportunity with bat and ball and enjoyed the experience. The highlight was winning the cup competition, the Pheonix Cup, in 1980. The knockout competition ended with a final against Hull University Employees at Hull Zingari's ground. It was on a Sunday. I came back from holiday to play and was glad I did. I hit 23 not out in a total of 96 for 3. It was too much for the Employees who finished on 68.

Innings over v Employees

My final spell of league cricket was in Cheshire. In 1987, I got a headship in Hartford, near Northwich. Next to the school was the village cricket ground. Despite being invited to open for Northwich in the Cheshire League, I opted for the Cheshire Competition with Hartford and didn't regret my decision. I batted top three and scored lots of runs. There were some decent cricketers and it was a standard which suited me considering I had little chance to practise.

Most teams were on the opposite side of the M62, around Knutsford and south Manchester. Burnage was perhaps the furthest. I opened the batting and was out first ball there once. I didn't bowl or take a catch and spent some time convincing my wife on returning home that it had been eight hours well-spent! Whenever I got a blob my stock excuse was that I had got the best ball of the day. I remember scoring 77 at Kerridge near Macclesfield, despite the distractions from the Woodford Air Show behind the bowler's arm. It was to be my personal best score. Sadly, a century remained elusive. I was left high and dry on 49 not out in the return. Having run a key player out I decided that the best course of action was to stay out there and by the time I had returned to the pavilion, moods had mellowed. Kerridge could count themselves unlucky to be taken advantage of to this extent. I cannot remember it happening to any other club in a season. I could have won the league batting prize in my first season but did not play enough times. I finished one game short. I moved on in 1995, away from Cheshire and league cricket. It had been an interesting journey with enough highs to look back on with pleasure.

# 15  Friendly Cricket

Many would claim that there isn't such a game and they may be right. Friendly games can come in various shapes and sizes. They can be every bit as absorbing and competitive as league stuff. There might be scores to settle and points to prove. Take games between staff and pupils. I have been involved in a few of these. They are usually played towards the end of term. The pupils have been practising and playing for weeks and see the chance to put one over on teachers who might have made their life a misery in class or around school. They believe that youthful energy will win the day. This is a dangerous mindset. They will ping the ball at your head but as the game wears on you can see the enthusiasm drain from them as their seniors turn the screw. I don't remember losing many, even the game where I opened ahead of a batting tail that began at three.

I've played alongside many a teacher who, once he squeezed back into the fading whites and dated jumpers, summoned up an inner strength as past glories flooded back. That 32 which saved the game at Nether Poppleton Seconds, the three wickets against St. Jimmy's College. Bob Clapp had rather more than that to look back on. He played for Somerset in the seventies alongside a young Ian Botham. Bob was a colleague at Rossall School, as was Guy Emmett who has been a professional player in Cheshire for many years. Many others have represented school, university and clubs and the pupils underestimated us at their peril.

# 16  Cricket Equipment

I've played a few sports over the years but none come anywhere near matching cricket for the range and complexity of its equipment. As a kid I managed with very little but when someone is spearing a solid spherical missile at you from twenty two yards away you need protection. So the abdominal guard was invented, commonly known as the 'box'. I bought my one and only box from the uniform shop at Giggleswick School in 1970 and it lasted me a cricketing lifetime. It was a bit like buying a packet of Durex in the chemist. I was pleased that the shop was empty and nervous about asking for one. I was immediately in two minds as to how to carry my box back across 'the Flat', a large concreted area at the heart of the school. Part of me was embarrassed to be seen carrying one, another regarding it as a symbol of my manhood. I strode as confidently as I could, box in hand. I etched my initials into the softer material round the outside and waited for a chance to try it on.

Making it stay in place proved problematic. I didn't have a proper undergarment, complete with pouch, until well into my adult career.  I just stuffed my box inside my pants, whereupon it took on a life of its own. There were no straps to attach round me so it slipped all over the place. Consequently, there would be a lot of fiddling between balls, as if a mouse had got down there and was scampering around. When it did come into its own, the ball thudded in to the groin and the effect was to send shock waves through my nether regions. Still, better than getting your balls crushed. It saved my bacon, or rather, my sausage, a few times along the way and I was entertaining thoughts of mounting it on a special plinth on retirement before an image of my wife came into my mind.

My box became the first thing to check in my cricket bag. Anything else could be borrowed but you were not predisposed to borrowing an item that had lived inside someone's underpants for long periods and not had a wash. In desperate circumstances, the communal box might be passed down the line from player to player, a withering detail for those committed to health and safety. I've known cricketers not bothered about what they stuff down their trousers but for many there's no escaping the fact that the pink object lying in front of them has been intimate with not one but several team-mates over the last couple of hours. Sometimes, it is still warm…Occasionally, I handled a warm one. It was a bit like sitting on the warm toilet seat in a public convenience. If you've got a practice ball, it fits nicely into it in your cricket bag. Trevor, my captain in Hull, had a couple of boxes and, one day, one of his children was looking at them with her friend. The friend asked what they were for, to which the answer came back, 'Daddy keeps his balls in them.'

These days cricketers of all ages tend to use their own equipment. Consequently, individual bags are more prevalent with some effectively large ones, nicknamed 'coffins'. The changing room has become a more hazardous place with players prone to turning ankles as they negotiate their way from the peg to the door or toilet. In the sixties and seventies we were accustomed to the one bag shared by the team. It would contain three pairs of batting pads, a pair of wicket keeping pads, several bats, several pairs of batting gloves, a pair of wicket keeping gloves and that pink plastic box. I remember that the wicket keeping pads were much bulkier. If wickets fell fast it was not unusual to see the next batsman approaching the crease uncomfortably, legs wider apart. It wasn't easy to move quickly in wicket keeping pads. The clatter of quick wickets was always a cue for merry hell in the changing room. The traditional calm went out of the window as equipment flew everywhere. By the end of August the cry went out, 'How the hell am I supposed to bat without a pair of gloves that fit me?' It is one of cricket's enduring mysteries. How can four pristine pairs at the start of May become five left-handed and one right-handed one by September?

Back in school days there could be a real mixed bag of equipment. By the time you got down to the Under 13's Third Team finding matching pads or two with the required number of straps could be a real problem. Bats might have a ripped grip or a split in the blade. If there were so few, you would pick up the one used by the outgoing batsman as you passed. Pimply gloves suffering from over-use developed holes in the lining. In the very early days they had a separate thumb protection on the end of an elastic strap which had to be wound round your hand. Many a time I got it the wrong way, leaving a thumb socket tantalisingly short of its destination.

I was always nervous immediately before going in so I preferred to open. Thus, I always got ready to bat in a familiar order. Jockstrap, box, thigh pad, left pad and right pad as one batsman was waiting ahead of me. Gloves were put on, left glove before right, as I walked into bat.

The star turn equipment-wise was the bat and there was no greater pleasure than choosing your own. Carved from pure willow, new bats were objects of beauty. The blade was smooth to the touch, with a hint of grain running through. You had to be careful not to get carried away with appearance as you cast your eye along the line in the shop. It was more about height and weight. Get that wrong and you'll get nowhere. I've looked on as a teacher at children from rich backgrounds wielding state of the art, top of the range full-size bats which they will never fully control. They could barely lift them.

The temptation to go out and hit balls was great but there was important preparation needed and it took time. The smell of linseed oil still holds fond memories. Pour a little on to a soft rag and start to rub into the virgin wood. As you do, the colour of the blade darkens. Cover the front and edges up to the splice. As it dried I practised off drives and pulls with an imaginary ball. Then it was time to apply more. It was a delicious, magical experience which died out as bats came covered with special protective coats. The second stage of preparation was 'knocking-in'. An old ball would be tapped repeatedly up and down the willow. Occasionally, you might come across a ball on the end of a stick, specially manufactured for this role. This was not an operation to rush.

I still have my cricket bats in the garage. They have survived many throwing out/tidying up sessions. Occasionally, they see the light of day such as when my two year-old grandson was wielding his first bat in the garden. He had just replicated the shot played by Chris Broad in the 1988 Bicentenary Test at Sydney, the one where he smashed his wickets, when I appeared with my blade. I swear that as I walked through the kitchen and in to the back garden, bat in hand, I was once again leaving the pavilion and entering the field of play. Fifty for four and a captain's knock needed.

On the back of each bat are faded scores from times past. Today they serve to remind me that I was once a half decent player. Many a time I have a quick glance as I'm searching for a piece of timber or a Phillips screw. Back in the day, it was part of the psychological part of my game. I imagined the wicket keeper bending down behind the stumps to face the spinner and coming eyeball to timber with the back of my blade. He would strain to read the details. *54 v Spartans 20/06, 59 v Sutton 5/07, 64\* v Kerridge 16/05.* The word would soon go round. 'This guy's good, you wanna see the back of his bat.'

My Slazenger V12 once belonged to Allan Lamb, the South African who played for Northamptonshire and England. From him it passed to Neil Mallender, another Northants player, then to John Batty at Hull Cricket Club. John kindly gave me it after taking him to a couple of cricket coaching courses in Hornsea. It was a heavy blade but I used it and had some success. I often wondered what story it could tell about its life in cricket. I had visions of Allan Lamb striding out purposefully at Lords, white helmet on head. He would be punching balls through midwicket down to the Mound Stand and taking risky airborne shots over fielders' heads, confident in his own ability. Then the baton would be passed on to Neil Mallender. With a batting average a shade over 17, Mallender would likely have used the middle much less than Lamb. With John Batty, who wouldn't have a bat contract, it would have lasted longer and travelled up and down the motorways and 'A' roads of Yorkshire. It may even have gone on tour but likely only to be used until the Thursday by which time intoxication and lack of sleep would have kicked in.

Replacing a bat's rubber grip was one of those quirky arts which never ceased to fascinate. The removal of the tatty cover followed by the magical positioning of its successor, first rolled inside out down a special stick marginally wider than the handle then transferred on to the bat before being rolled out along the handle. There was a real sense of satisfaction when it worked, as it usually did. I once performed the task in front of a class full of children enjoying quiet reading. Some watched on curiously above their books as I nonchalantly went about my business, a little too nonchalantly as it happened. Job done, I stood up and the class erupted as the bat bounced up and down, my tie stuck inside the new grip.

# 17 Scoring

Cricket scorers must rate pretty high up the list of sporting anoraks. As an activity, scoring ranks right up there with train spotting and stamp collecting in the geeky stakes. It is as far from rock n' roll and living on the edge as it is possible to be. Over the years numbers have dwindled but it is still possible to spot this hardy breed with sightings across the country from Canterbury to Chester-le-Street throughout the summer months. In the early part of the season they will usually be spotted wearing thick plumage to keep the biting winds and persistent rain at bay but as the temperatures rise, the outer coat falls off to reveal a brightly-coloured county top from the merchandise range and, often, a pair of unfashionable khaki shorts.

Recording a game of cricket ball by ball has survived the test of time since notches were cut in wood. It is comforting to know that in an age where technological advances have made things so easy, there are still people out there in good weather and bad resting a scorebook or clipboard on their laps with an impressive array of coloured pens and pencils to hand. Every now and then, the television cameras will focus on one of the species, prompting comments about days gone by and how good it is to see this ancient art perpetuating. The scorer will sit content in the knowledge that, whatever the state of play, there is always a response needed on paper to every single delivery. The modus operandi remains the same as in the black and white days. Superficially, you can only differentiate the sixties and the twenty-first century models by the earpiece which now allows a link to TMS or Sky via one of the ECB's commentary radios. Each and every moment of play is dutifully recorded. A dull session for the spectator can be manna from heaven for the scorer. There is always a statistical milestone to look forward to in every hour of play.

The records book will be to hand to cross refer, tucked away next to the flask. The most number of consecutive maiden overs in an afternoon session at Edgbaston when there is a 'J' in the month would send the anoraks home satisfied. There might not be anyone interested enough to convey the information to but that doesn't matter. There is still a feeling of inner contentment.

I appear to mock but, in truth, I am one of them. I have been absorbed by the gentle art of cricket scoring since those days back in the sixties when I stood on the small ladders inside Settle Cricket Club's scorebox and kept everyone up to date. I tried to score from the television but it was mighty frustrating with the breaks in coverage back then. You had hardly completed an over when you were off to Sandown Park or Wimbledon. Dad knew Arnold Whipp who did a lot of the television scoring for the BBC and he would often bring me examples of the sheets that he used.

Scorebooks come in all shapes and sizes. The basic model is a square shaped, card-backed variety usually light green. It was a start but nothing like the larger hard-backed versions. They were much-valued. They contained room for many more runs and overs. Each pristine page was approached with care. Details of the game would be entered first, across the top of the sheet.

Pencil was the best medium for me to use as mistakes could be easily rectified. Every ball had to be recorded in both the batting and bowling sections. Action was shown by symbols. A wide was registered with a cross, a no ball with a circle, a ball not scored off became a dot. The sheet filled almost imperceptibly as the game took hold, like an artist developing a painting stroke by stroke. There were rules to learn, of course, symbols to get used to. Oh, and you mustn't forget to record the times when batsmen started and finished their innings. It would all be pretty confusing to a non-cricket lover, like stumbling across some Egyptian hieroglyphics, but for the cricketing purist it was a work of art.

My finest hour lasted a whole week and confirmed my place in the cricket scorers' exclusive club. It was when I spent an entire family holiday scoring a six-day Test between England and Australia at the Oval in August 1972. I was eighteen-years old. Before you start thinking I should have been on the lash in Blackpool with my friends, or dating, I was a long way from that scenario. My emotional and sexual awakening was the last thing on my mind as I sat, pencil poised, for the start of play. I was more than happy to head to the ground each day as my dad visited museums and my mum and sister the shops. I was armed with my big, green, hard-backed scorebook, and every single delivery was duly recorded, from Barry Wood taking guard for England to Paul Sheahan and Rod Marsh knocking off the runs for Australia a week or so later. In between there was so much to record. The Chappell brothers both reached a century in the first innings and between them faced 493 balls. Each was recorded meticulously if frustratingly.

Then, when the game is over, the scorer attends to the averages. The batsman will be judged by the average number of runs per innings, the bowler by runs per wicket. The figures are added to the records for each player in the back of the book. I was denied the league batting trophy in Cheshire one year by holidays, too many of them to be precise. The number of games played was not enough for me to qualify. Averages produce statistics and cricket lovers have always thrived on those. The most famous stat is 99.94. You will know what I mean. Don Bradman needed just four in his last Test innings to finish with a career average of 100 and was out for nought at the Oval. I bet he felt like wrapping his cricket stump round his rainwater tank back home in New South Wales. It is a phenomenal average when the very best are judged on 60+ and a good Test average is 40+.

# 18 Captaincy

Learned books have been written about captaincy. Mike Brearley made a career out of it. There is much said about the pressures on England captains but it's nothing by comparison to the trials and tribulations of the Hull Zingari second team skipper never likely to lift a trophy. On the up side there is the kudos, the power it invests and the chance to use your tactical nous to shape the course of a game. If you get your batting order right, bowling changes go well and tactics in the field succeed, it is likely that you will taste victory. When the game has been won there is no better feeling. You can dine out on it for....well, about 48 hours until the next selection meeting. Victory soon becomes a fading memory as reality sets in.

This is the side of captaincy which tests the inner steel and nerves of even the strongest of people. I went into most selection meetings with a feeling of dread and a pin handy. The first team skipper would be sitting back after five minutes, job done. Another strong side on paper, mature, in-form sportsmen whose cars would have large boots able to transport the biggest of bags.

It got progressively more difficult from there as the third team skipper sought to put teams together. Tactics went out of the window. Practicalities took over. Clive is on a course in Uttoxeter and might be back in time. Rich is on nights but might be able to play if the game is at home. Jim's wife's baby is due late Friday, or it might go into Saturday. He'd like to play if possible. Names melted away, others had question marks added to them. Were there enough cars to get the third team to Londesborough Park? The third team almost resembled a crèche on occasions. Juniors may possess talent and energy but they can't drive. They don't buy rounds of drinks either.

From Wednesday, the phone calls begin. I would have the first team skipper on to me, regretting the loss of one of the star batsmen due to a pulled muscle in the gym. Before I had chance to offer a replacement, he would be straight in with his preferred choice. Inevitably, it would be one of my key players. I just knew that the promotion would result in my player batting nine or below and not bowling when I would have him five or bowling ten overs minimum. Before the week was over, negotiations would open with the third team skipper who could be a stubborn old beggar. I might have to release a qualified driver. By Friday night, panic could have set in. In the end, I might resort to my own pool of talent and ring up formers pupils who had once played for me as eleven year olds. Now they are alongside me in an adult dressing room where swearing and rude comments are par for the course. Come match day, I am vowing to make this my last season as captain and dreading the moment when Mrs. Mitchell reads the telephone bill.

Before the toss, I always said little to the opposing captain. I found it best that way. This was an approach based on experience. If he said they had a good team I believed him, if they had a poor team I immediately thought he was lying. Either way, I could easily psyche myself out before a ball had been bowled. The toss at amateur league level was poles apart from the pro-game where match conditions would have been assessed in the days leading up to the game and advice sought from a range of experts from the coach downwards.

On a number of occasions I've been to the middle with only four or five players in sight, particularly away from home. In the days before mobiles it was difficult to find out where the others were. Cars didn't have sat navs and had a habit of going in the wrong direction or getting stuck in holiday traffic. You might want to field ordinarily, and go for the draw, but it looked like batting was the only option and hope the rest got there in time. If the other skipper called correctly and asked you to field you were in trouble. In those situations I was virtually praying as the coin flipped. As a rule I always called 'heads' after reading somewhere that coins come down on 'heads' marginally more than 'tails'. Decisions made, I would indicate to the rest with a mimed shot or twirl of the arm. In international games, a former player will stand by on the pitch with microphone ready for a comment or two from each captain. Just imagine one in our games,

*You've won the toss and inserted the opposition, David. Tell us your thinking.*

*Well, at the moment Nass I've got five players.*

On returning to the pavilion I would confirm the batting order as far down as I was prepared to go and then let the rest unfold. There would inevitably be greater issues to deal with.

Captaincy for home matches carried the responsibility of the team teas. Tactics over ninety overs paled into insignificance compared with the responsibility of getting the teas right. It usually involved a roster of 'volunteers'. As an opening batsman, there have been times when I have walked towards the square nervously glancing across to the entrance, hoping to see tea and helpers arriving. The urn had to be turned on in good time. Some were antique pieces that required a long time to come to the boil. They made strange gurgling noises and steam hissed out in all directions. A bit like a few cricketers I've played with. Mrs. Mitchell took her turn providing food for teas. They were high quality. Her speciality was homemade buns with icing and a cherry on top. Our fast bowler at Hull always played with intensity and you dropped a catch off him at your peril...but he couldn't resist an iced bun!

After the game, you had to make sure that subs were collected, umpires paid, kit gathered up and places locked up. Then you had to fraternise with opposition who had just thumped you whilst your team mates retired to a corner and had a good time. You could guarantee that the ones left from the opposition were the least sociable or those who had just taken a 'five for' or scored a fifty. Eventually, you were relieved and could return home for a couple of days respite before that next selection meeting.

# 19  Life On Tour

Every now and then the regular pattern of play would be interrupted by that traditional cricket activity, going on tour. This involved a week of drinking and fun with the minor inconvenience of a game played each day. It was similar to the cricket festivals at school but with hardened, experienced party animals. By the end of the week, selection options became fewer in number as first one player, then another, would declare themselves unavailable and slope off to a corner to sleep indefinitely. I recall a team mate who spent the night drinking, followed by a morning golf match. He sacrificed lunch in order to refresh himself for the afternoon game against St. Margaret's in Kent. On awakening quarter of an hour before the start, he was mortified to learn he had been left out by the mean-spirited, Boycott-worshipping tour organiser.

His drinking partner of the night before was spotted asleep on the stairs at quarter to eight the following morning, a nap which enabled him to fulfil the golf commitment and play cricket. On the final evening he accompanied the opening batsman into Margate. They liaised with two frauleins and, returning to the hotel, a lamp post suddenly leapt out in front of them. The opening batsman was left trailing as his friend decided to get as far away as possible from a crashed, uninsured car and two bewildered German girls. The tour ended with a game in Nottinghamshire on the way back to Hull. Unfortunately, the club kit was secure in the boot of the crashed car, now in a Kent Constabulary compound. The club skipper intervened and persuaded them to release the kit but the team arrived in Notts with eight players, neatly matching the eight opposition players. The missing tourist rang during the tea interval declaring his unavailability for cricket that day.

I stayed with family, away from trouble. I took my college mate Marshy one year. He was a Kent boy and became the only person I know who started a ciggy, went into bat and came back in time to finish it. That was at Dover. I had my fifteen minutes of fame, a seven-for against Broadstairs and a fifty at St. Margaret's. I'm probably the only player from the club to play for and against us on the same tour.

The Northern Tour with the Cryptics was quite different. This was a club whose members were former public school boys. For years I played for them. For a week each August I joined Knights of the realm, double-barrelled names and players with anything up to four initials. There were some posh players and posh and strange team names in the public school world. We came up against the Yorkshire Gentlemen and the Craven Gentlemen. Elsewhere were teams with wonderful names such as the Stragglers of Asia, the Pink Elephants and the Hampshire Hogs.

Blazers were worn at the toss, a bell would be rung to signal the start of play, lunch and tea would be leisurely. It was all very civilised with due diligence paid to the niceties of cricket. There was none of this fielding first business on winning the toss. It was traditional to bat first and head to a challenging declaration somewhere mid-afternoon taking the match to an exciting conclusion in the twenty overs of the last hour. It was not unusual for teams to lend each other players to make up eleven.

Batsmen with fancy names and colourful caps vied with bowlers who had film star looking girlfriends and posh cars on the boundary edge. The very old boys would still turn out, batting at number eleven and fielding at first slip so they didn't have to run. School ties would hold up their trousers. A cravat displaying the club or former school colours would add a touch of class. By the conclusion, the shadows would have lengthened and the evening gloom gathered round players, families and friends quaffing beer and wine in no rush to leave the bosom of their own kith and kin. Chat would centre round trips to visit great aunts on the south coast, golf or life in the financial or legal professions. There was an old-fashioned feel to the occasion. You were careful not to drop your h's.

Tuesday and Wednesday were the days for that great novelty item, the two-day game. The opposition were the Durham Pilgrims, the venue Castle Eden cricket club. The Pilgrims had a base centred around Durham School but brought in local league players and the odd professional from the North Yorkshire and South Durham league. These were the days well before the county was granted first-class status but the standard was invariably very high. We played against some of the Durham's most promising young talent, including Mike Roseberry and the Weston brothers. Rob Andrew was another. For an international rugby player, he was a more than decent cricketer. I would love to have been not out overnight, turning away the fourth beer because there was a job to do in the morning. It happened once which I was really pleased about. I was out in the first over next morning.

# 20  Televised Cricket

My appetite for cricket in the sixties was further fed by a diet of televised coverage which was patchy compared to today's output but all that I knew at the time. On 24th July 1965, for instance, twenty minutes was sandwiched between the news and the Royal Tournament. The days of Sky devoting a whole channel to the sport and BT throwing big money at the game were a long way off. My earliest recollections are black and white ones. The BBC would show Test matches. There would be little build-up ahead of the day's play. I had to wait patiently as the test card was on the screen accompanied by light music. This was a television test signal typically played when the transmitter was active but no programme being broadcast. In the middle was an eight-year-old girl playing noughts and crosses on a blackboard with a toy clown. Nowadays we would be watching 'Homes Under the Hammer' or some cookery programme but we weren't privy to a constant diet of television back then. The cricket coverage might start at five to eleven, five minutes before play. Then, following a brief introduction from the studio announcer with the plummy voice, it was straight into 'Soul Limbo' by Booker T and the MGs. I kept my fingers crossed and the nerves jangled through the credits. My heart sank when the live pictures showed covers spread across the pitch, a sure sign that I would have to wait longer to watch play.

The welcoming voice was likely to be Peter West. Dapper, hair parted to one side with Brylcream, pipe doubtless sticking out of his top jacket pocket. West's expertise transcended other sports, particularly rugby union. His was a versatility that extended to presenting 'Come Dancing', the early form of 'Strictly'. Alongside him in the commentary box were the likes of Brian Johnston, Richie

Benaud, Jim Laker and Denis Compton. West would likely be perched on top of one of the stands, out in the open.

Very often, coverage began sometime after the play had started. Half past eleven might be half an hour into play. Another frustration was the clash with other sports, particularly racing or Wimbledon. On Saturdays, cricket would take its place within a package of sports on the late-lamented 'Grandstand'. Racing was particularly annoying, partly because I had no interest in it but with races starting every half hour or so there wasn't much time for cricket coverage in between before we headed back to Peter O'Sullivan for the build up to the ten past four at Newbury. You were practically willing him to wind up after the race so you could get back to the cricket. If rain held up play, there was a good reason to go to other sport. Otherwise, a caption and music was all we had while they waited for the sun to come out. These days, we would get protracted conversations and action from previous matches. Anyone under the age of thirty would find it difficult to believe that coverage could be so sporadic. They would have likely come into watching twenty years ago when Channel 4 won the right to cover and transformed our viewing, a mantle taken on by Sky and BT.

The first televised action that stuck in my mind was a Test match at Lords in 1963. Skipper Colin Cowdrey fended off a bouncer from West Indian quick Wes Hall and broke his wrist. When Derek Shackleton was run out in the last over, England needed six to win with one wicket left and two balls to survive. Cowdrey returned, arm in plaster and watched from the other end as David Allen blocked the last two balls for a draw. It was definitely a match that formed part of my cricketing education. I was engrossed.

Another clear memory was from 1968 when BBC Wales captured the greatest over in cricket. Garry Sobers hit Malcolm Nash to all parts of Swansea as he struck six sixes in one over. Having been told by the producers of 'Grandstand' to shut down the cameras, a guy called John Norman kept them going as they wanted to watch Sobers through a fixed lens and further practice their cricket coverage. With Wilf Wooler's commentary, the film had been sold to fifteen countries by the next day.

Roses Matches were often covered by Granada or Yorkshire TV, both at Old Trafford and Headingley. Those were the days before grounds had a sponsor's name attached in front of them. Compared to Sobers antics, there was quite a bit of attritional cricket. These were the days before white ball cricket bred a type of batsman incapable of playing a lengthy innings. Neither side wanted to yield to their greatest foe and, of course, ITV coverage was interrupted by adverts.

The one-day game began to appear with Gillette Cup games on Wednesdays and the Sunday afternoon matches played by the International Cavaliers. I loved watching these games on BBC2. The cricket schedule was a lot simpler back then. Sunday was nominally a rest day from Test Matches which always started on Thursday, and from the County Championship. This spawned a whole raft of friendly matches. County beneficiaries used Sundays for matches at local clubs. The International Cavaliers emerged between 1965 and 1970 when former England players Denis Compton and Godfrey Evans arranged 40 over one-day games. They were a kind of precursor of teams like Lashings and Old England where international players got together to encourage local cricket. The BBC televised the games and spectators were able to see a wide range of former players at county grounds. Modern coloured outfits were noticeably absent back then. Whites were the order of the day. The events attracted legendary players. Ted Dexter once wrote about such a side which contained Sobers, Compton and Graeme Pollock. 'I was only able to creep in at six or seven.' It might be the Cavaliers v The Duke of Norfolk's XI or Oxford University Past and Present. Touring Test teams occasionally featured. One player I happen to remember was Rhodesia-born Fred Goldstein, a hard-hitting opening batsman. The popularity of the matches led to an increase in one-day cricket in England.

The John Player County League began in 1969 and the Cavaliers were disbanded the following year.

# 21  Watching Test Cricket Live

A day at the cricket is not to be taken half-heartedly. There is much to consider and plan, not least the contents of the food hamper. A supermarket sweep later and you have stocked up with enough Scotch eggs and pork pies to outdo your friends. Never mind salad and granary bars. Sandwiches, crisps, sausage rolls, pasties and chocolate bars are the order of the day at the cricket. All disappear into a seemingly bottomless bag, ready to be revealed at regular intervals like a card from a hand of knock out whist. *'A sausage roll, eh? I can trump that'*... produces giant sausage roll. There is always way more food than you are likely to eat in any normal day at home and a flask filled with coffee that really needs to be supped by the end of the lunch period before it goes cool. There may just be room for a small pair of binoculars and the paper. A cushion becomes particularly important when the scoring rate dips under three an over while an umbrella is an optional extra on days when rain threatens.

The excitement mounts as you walk to the ground, laden down with your heavy backpack which is given over for inspection by the security guards at the gate. They are actually salivating by the time they've reached the bottom. Woe betide you try to smuggle alcohol in. The ground authorities would rather you paid the extortionate prices inside. On the way to my seat I will look at people, trying to recognise one or even a cricket club motif on a jumper or t-shirt. Once at the chosen spot, it is time to take stock of your view for the day, assess how the sun's path will affect you, what chance there is of an appearance on television and how easy it will be to get to the toilet. In front of you is a playing area just heaving with people. That is the way of it these days. Apart from the players and coaches, the ever-growing media bandwagon confirm their authenticity with official-looking lanyards draped around their necks. The two teams will be playing football for a time, before fielding practice. I never understood that. You can't imagine Manchester United playing a game of tip and run before the City derby.

Your binoculars will allow you to identify more famous faces on the field than friends without them. *'That's Vic Marks there, just next to Mark Nicholas. Can you see? He looks like he's put a bit of weight on. Oh, and Vaughny. Can you see him?'*

Who's that talking to Aggers?

*It's Graham Smith... or is it Ed Smith?*

If they aren't doing interviews, these guys and gals will be chatting to each other about times past or having an important conversation on phones, probably to each other. Each will have a cluster of sound and camera technicians hovering around them. Back at the start of my half century, there would barely have been anyone beyond the players who will actually have been practising cricket.

If you are there on day one, which I liked to be, there was the excitement of the toss. One of the ex-cricketers will supervise proceedings. There are tense moments as the coin flicks airborne. I so want England to bat first on my day at the Test. I think it has happened more often than not. It used to be a mystery for a short while then the plummy-voiced announcer would reveal all. Now there are interviews with the two captains through a sound system strong enough to carry to the very furthest seats.

Depending on the venue, you know where the 'weather' is coming from. The weather forecasts have been studied with a fine-toothed comb for days before. It's a thrilling feeling when you know there will be a clear day and England are batting. Otherwise, David Lloyd will be heard saying, 'It's not looking good over Bill's back yard' as he gazes out across Manchester. There was only once when play was virtually wiped out to just a few overs. The Aussies were at Old Trafford. There was financial compensation but it was small comfort.

The atmosphere is cranked up over the final ten minutes before play. The big screens show packages of cricket highlights accompanied by a frenzied soundtrack. The ubiquitous adverts are there. Then, just as you thought you couldn't take any more excitement, it's time for 'Jerusalem'. William Blake's stirring words are accompanied by young people waving flags in their escort for the players. Play about to start and you're anxious for the toilet due to all the excitement. It's all many moons away from my early live watching. I blame Sky.

There is always a thrill as the players come on. There's nothing better than two England batsmen following the Australians out on day one. The atmosphere around is one of expectation. It is early days and none of us know what kind of day will take shape. It doesn't take long for the first items to emerge from the lunch bag. It is ten past eleven, still an hour and more from normal lunchtime in the real world. Somehow, it doesn't matter when you are at the cricket. You are totally in control of your input. There will be a glance across from your friends, possibly an admiring one if you have something that they omitted. They will make a mental note to include one next time.

By now, the beer is starting to flow on the terraces, into mouths and down steps. As the day wears on, spectators will think nothing of making the long walk from seat E234 or J179 in the middle of the row at the top tier of the stand down to a distant beer outlet which looks the size of a toy. They return twenty five minutes later with four plastic pint glasses precariously held together by a cardboard 'crate'. Not one holds the same amount that was in when the return journey began. The drinks are passed along from a standing position to cries of 'SI' DOWN!', that universal call of the cricket follower. Within no time at all, what is left of the pints has been drunk and the process starts again.

I used to take a large radio to the cricket. It attracted a lot of attention from those around me. Its inclusion always cut down the amount of food in the bag but it provided the commentary from Test Match Special and let you, knowingly, tell those who jibed some salient background details about the movement of the ball or why mid-off is hobbling. You were immediately in a better place than others. More recently, the ECB have made the ear pieces available. Amongst other things, they have allowed Bumble to have a conversation with an unsuspecting fan in Block G who has been highlighted by the television.

By lunchtime, lunch has well and truly disappeared, as has half of tea. It is time for that traditional custom – the walk around the ground. I have to say that this has got more difficult over the years. At Leeds and Manchester you could stroll with ease, visit the bookshop or the museum, watch a player or two in the nets and come back in good time with an ice cream. It just seems to have got busier and busier at the Test match. There is less space to move in. More people sell beer, more sell burgers. The public are invited to take part in activities with a cricketing theme. These days, the circular route is full of obstacles.

By mid-afternoon we look across to the popular stand and see the latest attempt on the world record for the longest plastic snake. Hundreds of empty plastic beer 'glasses' are gathered and joined together. Punters come from all directions with their own contributions. As the snake gets longer, attention turns away from the cricket, particularly if there is little happening on the field. At Old Trafford in 2017, the snake stretched all the way from row one at the front to the back of the stand. As the last few were put in place, there was a spontaneous round of applause from around the ground and a chorus of 'God Save The Queen.' There was then a moment as eighty people wondered what to do next with the part they were holding up before the whole sculpture was thrown into the air and came tumbling down in many directions. Oh, how the cheers rang out.

By now we could be well into the sport within the sport, heckling the fielder. There is nothing a lubricated mass of cricket watchers like more than baiting a fielder in front of them. Eight thousand Western Terracers at Headingley will join in as one and heaven help the poor player who spills a catch or misfields in full view. There will be no second chance given. It does not help if the player is from Lancashire, Essex, Middlesex or Surrey. I remember Essex captain, Keith Fletcher, struggling to get bat on ball for England at Headingley. An announcement came up regarding a car that was illegally parked. One wag shouted, 'It can't be Fletcher's, he can't drive!' If the player has taken a Yorkshire hero's place in the England side he needs to be above rebuke. Like a pack of wolves, they move in for the kill, sensing vulnerability, a chink in the armour. The player, in return, can either ignore the comments or play to the crowd. The second reaction usually goes down better. He is then seen as a good sport. Every touch will be accompanied by a drunken cheer from the packed terraces behind. A small wave will trigger a cacophony of sound. The sub-plot gathers momentum as the lubrication takes greater effect.

Most of the remaining food is scoffed at tea time. This might be at twenty to four. No one eats their tea at twenty to four except on the cricket grounds of England. More Scotch Eggs and Pork Pies are being tucked away. By the end of the day all sorts will have happened in your area. It will be scattered with tiny bits of paper from the Mexican Wave. You will have made new friends with Dave and Bob from Derby. Next to them will be Tony from Cleckheaton who you think you might have played against many seasons ago. At Old Trafford in 2017 I was sitting next to the son of a pupil I had taught in Hull in the seventies. That was a shock. The language will have got riper as the beer kicked in and the banter will be directed at anyone and everyone who provides ripe material. Your food will likely have gone and you will be feeling tired after a day in the sun. Chairs begin to empty as occupants leave early to get ahead of the crowds. I could never quite understand that. Finally, the last ball is followed by announcements concerning tomorrow's play and it is time to go back into everyday life.

# 22  Test Match Special

Over the years I have become a master at keeping up with the game as well as doing jobs. With television you become skilled in getting on with things in other rooms and walking to a vantage point to see the next ball being bowled. A quick bowler will allow you just a few more seconds out of sight. With a spinner it is tricky. So, I can wash up and watch simultaneously, walking backwards and forwards every minute or so. Ironing is more straightforward because you can set up in front of the screen and take your time. I can write at my computer and automatically turn to the screen as the bowler runs in. A sixth sense garnered over the years has produced an ability to turn just at the right moment.

With radio it is quite different. It is easier to become more absorbed because the radio is portable. I have listened in to whole sessions on the radio while working in the garage or decorating the outside of houses. The real skill here is to combine painting, cricket and following the course of the sun round the house, whilst ensuring that you come down for refreshment during the lunch and tea breaks. Care is needed when celebrating landmarks at the top of a ladder. I remember a Gooch triple hundred where I almost got carried away with myself and could easily have ended up in Hull infirmary.

Test Match Special has been one of the most pleasurable constants of my half century. People mutter that it's not as it used to be but, let's face it, a pretty special commentary team has departed to take up celestial duties in the heavenly commentary box.…John Arlott, Brian Johnson, Christopher Martin-Jenkins, Alan Gibson, Don Mosey, Trevor Bailey, Fred Trueman and Bill Frindall. That is an impressive list and I have listened to them talking for longer periods of time than some of my family.

TMS gives me my own personal invite into a conversation with no idea as to how it will develop. Periods of play are interspersed with anecdotes, quirks and stats. I could not wait for Ollie Pope to arrive at the crease for his England debut in 2018 and hear how many Olivers have represented England or alternative clerical surnames for that matter. I have listened here, there and everywhere - at the top of a ladder, under bedclothes, at the actual match, in the car, in the garage, whilst working and whilst watching the match on television. That is a good way. Sound turned down, radio tuned in.

Radios have come and gone, splashed with paint, muddied with garden soil-all in the name of keeping up with the cricket and enjoying the banter. The future of ball by ball radio coverage has come under threat from time to time but it has stood the test.

Bizarrely it is a programme which can be at its most absorbing when the rain stops play. Here lies one of its strengths. Conversation, pure and simple. Not just the current game but any manner of things as the thread gets longer, weaving in wonderful cricketing stories. 'Have I told you my Glenn Turner story?' Aggers will say and then we are deflected off down a different tangent. And with the wonder of social media it is now possible to even join in that conversation, sending a message or making a point which is received instantaneously.

# 23  Shipping Forecast

As long as I can remember, live coverage on long wave has been interrupted by the shipping forecast. Frustrating though it is, we have to concede the importance to the fishing community of hearing updates at set times on a clear frequency. Much of the time it matters not. On a rain-interrupted period – fine, during a dull period of play – a minor inconvenience, clashing with a drinks break – perfect. Sometimes we might miss a fifty, a century or a wicket. Back in January 2011 it mattered rather more. England cricket fans listened in to coverage of the Ashes series from Sydney. As England approached victory in both match and series, we went to the shipping forecast. We listened with growing impatience as weather news came through from Cromarty, Dogger and German Bight. Across the world, Australia's last batsman, Michael Beer, was bowled by Chris Tremlett and the celebrations had already kicked off by the time coverage resumed. It had been twenty-four long years since the last time England had won in Australia. An unfortunate piece of timing but what makes it all the more extraordinary is that it was the third time in the series that England's winning moment had been missed for this reason. Previously, it had happened in the Second Test at Adelaide and the Fourth Test at Melbourne. England's moment in each came during the 00.48 a.m. update. Why wasn't the shipping forecast delayed? Well, apparently, there has to be at least six hours' notice given. I have a vision of a cricket-mad sea captain sitting on the bridge in perfect weather conditions, pipe dangling from mouth, cap at an angle. He is anticipating the result as much as we are when…..'And now for the shipping forecast.'

# 24 The Scorecard Seller

Firmly rooted in cricket culture is the scorecard seller. He, and it was invariably a he, would appear at regular points through the day with bag over one shoulder containing the A5 size cardboard scorecards. You would hear him before you saw him. You would catch the guttural cry every minute or so, 'scoreCARD!' The first syllable was barely heard at times, all the emphasis being placed on the second. Call by call it would get gradually louder as the seller neared your position.

Various advertisements would feature on the cover, along with relevant match details, of course, while inside were the teams along with barely enough space to fill in the nature of dismissals and runs scored. I would go for something like 'ct 8 b 11'. The sellers' first tour of the ground would be early on day one when the inside was free of any updates, a pristine copy just waiting for your fair hand to first of all part with money then keep the details up to date. As the match developed, wickets would fall and further editions would contain printed details. For me, it was all about getting one of the first batch because your own additions never quite looked as good when put alongside the updates.

Scorecard sellers were a dedicated bunch. Rarely did they watch the play. Instead, their eyes were continually scanning the crowd, looking for a hint of a buyer. Maybe a word here or a raised arm there would indicate that a sale was imminent. They wandered up the steps between blocks of seats looking left and right …'scoreCARD!' As the day wore on, the scorecard seller's lot became a more difficult one. The effect of alcohol, or even a dull passage of play, would prompt playful banter from the crowd. This was not the time to have to pass a card across a few people or struggle to get the right change. 'SI' DOWN!' would ring out. It was wasted energy from the barrackers. The scorecard sellers were impervious to criticism. It mattered not what was happening on the field behind them. There could be a century approaching or a hat trick ball. The sellers never flinched. Maybe a wry smile would appear but nothing stopped their work. Not even, the repeated cries of 'SI'DOWN!' as views were obscured. The arrival of the scorecard sellers brought out Yorkshire humour at its best from the spectators. It never seemed to affect our dedicated bunch.

# 25 Playing on the outfield

One of the great joys of watching professional cricket was the chance to walk and play on the cricket field during lunch and tea breaks. The ground was the preserve of the cricket fan at these times. As the clock ticked towards the intervals children in all parts would turn their attention away from the action and on to what would happen when they got out there themselves. Clutching equipment, they would be visibly itching to run on and take their place on the outfield. For children used to the back road or the rough patch behind the rugby hut this was a joyous and rather surreal experience.

Within moments of the umpire calling 'OVER AND LUNCH', the outfield would become awash with colour and action as multiple games kicked into life. Stumps would have been pitched if you had come well-prepared. Clothing would act as an alternative. Game upon game would take place with over-exuberant hits peppering the crowd in the front rows of seats. The action was often a welcome diversion through the breaks for spectators. One game would merge into the next and by the time the players returned, the young fans would hopefully have had the chance to bat, ball and field on the hallowed ground. Adults, meanwhile, would drift on to the ground and make their way to the square. Those first few steps are magical. Your lawn was never like this. The ground feels so firm-bodied, the grass close-cropped. You turn and see the terraces behind you. On the larger grounds you gaze upward into the massive stands and start to imagine what it must be like to be part of the action. For twenty minutes you can believe what it is like to be a player.

Inevitably, adults are drawn towards centre stage. Although cordoned off, you could still wander up and gaze knowingly across the few yards of land where, just a few minutes ago, your heroes were playing. People for whom cutting the lawn is a weekly chore now stand transfixed by a strip of turf twenty-two yards long. A brush and rake take on a whole new meaning as the ground staff go about their business. There are footholds to study and opinions to express about that rough patch that was developing outside leg stump. There is a position to take up behind the stump holes, imaginary bat tapping the ground as you look down to the opposite end and the bowler coming in. It is as close as you might get to the real thing. Turning back to our seats it is just possible to cut off all the others around us and envisage just ourselves and ten others fielding. We might be hurried along by stewards as we saunter across the final few yards to the edge but no one can take away the pleasure of a few minutes in cricketing heaven.

# 26  Beach Cricket

On our Ruby Wedding anniversary in July 2018, the family played beach cricket. It is a fascinating exercise to watch how your loved ones adapt and react to the developing game on the sand. The experience convinced me that beach cricket is as exciting today as it was back in the sixties when it was an accepted part of holidays at Whitby, Scarborough and Bridlington. Fifteen years later I was playing league cricket in all those towns.

Third Test, Bridlington Beach 1961.

There were so many factors to take into consideration in beach cricket. The size of space available, the texture of sand and tide times are all crucial, particularly the last one. A rapidly advancing tide can catch boundary fielders unawares. It is virtually impossible to satisfy every participant's needs. Aunties and cousins arranged in far flung positions will soon get bored if the action on the pitch has a Test match Boycott-esque flavour. To satisfy the sport for all ethic, you need a bowler who can toss the ball invitingly and a batsman able to send it high and long to test the out fielders. The result is a two-fold bout of screaming. The first occurs as half a dozen or so see the trajectory broadly bringing the ball in their direction and panic sets in. The second happens when said ball is dropped. Cue mayhem and mass frivolity.

For the first time in my beach career I tried to video action as I stood as umpire. This was on my phone. Son bowled to father who hit ball out to mother…who dropped it time and again. *Dad caught Mum bowled Son* would have rivalled *Lillee caught Willey bowled Dilley*. It would have gone down in the annals of family videos. Mum didn't play ball so to speak. It is not the first time that I have filmed action from the umpire's position. I was once filming in a Surrey garden after a wedding when the batsman struck a ball horizontally and firmly straight at me. Keeping the film going I stuck out a hand and caught the ball in front of the lens. It is a moment still talked about when we get together. It could well be the moment I get remembered for.

Second Test, Whitby Beach 1962. Janet promoted from gulley to wicketkeeper

# 27  Overseas Players

One of the more obvious changes in my cricketing lifetime has been the role played by professional cricketers from abroad. Nowadays, overseas stars jet in and out of county sides for just a few weeks. T20 specialists might play in that competition only. Indian Premier League cricketers miss the start of the season and international tour commitments can take players away from counties for large chunks of time. We are also in the age of the multiple-county cricketer. Take Marcus North, for instance. The Australian played for six English counties in less than a decade from 2004. Players are constantly on the move these days. Countries' Boards take firm control and it contrasts significantly with the stability offered by overseas signings a generation and more ago.

Nowhere has the change been more evident than at Yorkshire. My home county proudly resisted bringing in from abroad for years, despite Lord Hawke having been born in Gainsborough, Lincolnshire. The committee remained steadfast about the rule stating that players born outside the boundaries could not feature. Twenty-four years ago, they relented and signed an overseas pro for the first time. It was 19 year-old Sachin Tendulkar. He experienced cold of the like he had never imagined and resorted to multiple jumpers. Others followed Tendulkar until it became normal and expected for the White Rose to sign an overseas player. The 2017 season was positively frantic. Travis Head was signed but the deal fell through due to Australia 'A's tour of South Africa. The tour never went ahead because of the Australian pay dispute. Peter Handscomb signed as the main overseas player. Another Aussie, Shaun Marsh, was added for the T20 and stayed on for a Championship match before the West Indian opener Kraigg Brathwaite arrived for the last two games. Oh, by the way, there was also Pakistan's Champions Trophy-winning captain,

Sarfraz Ahmed, who played five T20 games before being recalled by his country in the Independence Cup!

Of all Yorkshire's successive overseas players, Australian Darren Lehmann has shone bright. In seven seasons, he averaged 68.76 with the bat. His final innings of 339 was just two runs short of the highest score ever made for the club.

Gloucestershire were particularly well-served by overseas stars. South African, Mike Procter, played for fourteen seasons, five as captain. With a Test career denied by apartheid, Procter gave everything for his county. He amassed 14,441 runs and 833 wickets. He was so good that his team were dubbed 'Proctershire'. West Indian fast bowler, Courtney Walsh, spent eleven years with the county, three as captain. Gloucestershire finished rock bottom in his first season but over the next two he took 203 wickets at nineteen and his side finished third, then second. Others have won more silverware but Walsh was always loyal to the cause. Thanks to Clive Rice and Richard Hadlee, Nottinghamshire became double championship winners after sixty years searching for honours. Both were connected with the club for over a decade and exploited over-grassed Trent Bridge wickets.

Players such as these came and stayed, season after season. They were available throughout a season. They attracted many more fans as the television coverage increased. They gave themselves time to weave into the fabric of their county's history and into the hearts of the supporters. Clive Lloyd at Lancashire, Joel Garner at Somerset, Allan Donald at Warwickshire.

One of the most ambitious journeys to a ground was made by David Miller in 2017. It was 6000 miles long. Miller played for South Africa 'A' in the academic city of Potchefstroom. The journey was far from academic, involving helicopter, aeroplane, car and foot. Twenty-seven hours later he lined up for Glamorgan in Cardiff. Miller didn't have to bat or bowl as Glamorgan eased home by nine wickets in their T20 quarter-final against Leicestershire.

# 28 Putting a Spin on it

As a former slow bowler, there's nothing better than watching the course of a game changed by spin bowlers. In the modern game, they have come back into fashion, particularly valuable in T20 cricket. Traditionally spinners risked being slogged if they strayed but teams around the world are using them as potent weapons in their armoury. They keep run rates down and serve to tease batsmen in the early overs where the power play limits the defensive fields. It has not always been the case. Too often through my cricketing life they have been used to get a breakthrough, to give quick bowlers a rest or improve over rates. This has happened from school cricket all the way to Test matches.

Through more than enough cricket seasons, I have had to settle for watching a diet of mediums and quicks bowling over after remorseless over. The hours grind past with pitiful over rates and it is all pretty samey. There is no better example that the West Indies teams of the seventies and eighties. The country that produced Valentine, Ramadhin, Gibbs and Sobers gained world dominance through the quickest bowling attack ever seen. Michael Holding, Andy Roberts, Malcolm Marshall, Colin Croft and Joel Garner. Yes, it was an attack of exceptional quality but it allowed little opportunity for variety. One would be rested, another would move in. There was no respite for batsman or spectator.

Contrast that with the Indian team of the sixties and seventies. Sub-continent conditions favour spin and India had four world-class bowlers at the same time. Their names were a nightmare for scorers who would have to reach for the pencil sharpener when Srinivasaraghavan Venkataraghavan or Bhagwath Chandrasekhar came on to bowl. Venkat, the moustachioed off spinner, would characteristically sweep his hair out of his eyes before

96

starting an angular run. Chandra's long, bouncing run-up would be followed by leg breaks, sharply-spinning googlies and vicious top spinners. He took 6 for 38 at the Oval in 1971, giving India their first series win in England. At a young age, polio had withered Chandra's left arm but he made the most of his right and was India's match winner on many occasions. EAS Prasanna was a master of flight, often out-thinking batsmen before the ball had left his hand. And then there was Bishen Bedi. He of the many-coloured turbans. Slow left arm and as pure a bowler as I have seen. Flight, loop and spin were key to his armoury. I have been Bishen Bedi for hours in the back garden and on the street, trying to perfect that smooth delivery as he glided in.

There couldn't be a greater contrast between the bowling attacks of those two great countries. In my street games I mimicked all styles. There was the pure excitement of a fast run in and full-on delivery followed by the dull clang as the ball hit the oil tank wicket. If I wanted guile and magic I turned to spin and from those early days it was always the type of bowling which fascinated me. As a left hander by nature I was naturally drawn to Bedi but also Derek Underwood who destroyed the Aussies on a wet Oval pitch in 1968. His was a slightly longer, brisker run-up and delivery. I felt that when I was these two I was the real deal. None of my mates could do that. None of them were left handed. I occasionally experimented with the style of John Gleeson, who perfected an unorthodox grip by bowling at a gum tree in Australia. His finger grip was a struggle to perfect and more than once I risked a dislocation. Gleeson flummoxed batsmen in the early days. As they worked him out, his influence waned and a strike rate of a wicket every 95 balls was nothing special. Then there was Robin Hobbs. Nothing about Essex was boring and straightforward in the sixties and seventies. They had a side full of characters and in Hobbs they had the only regular leg-break bowler in the County Championship. He retired disillusioned with the way the game was going.

One point in spinning history stands out on its own. It was one of those sporting moments in time which just stunned all who saw it. I remember Spurs goalkeeper Pat Jennings scoring against Manchester United in the 1967 Charity Shield Final and just a year or so later Bob Beamon breaking the world long jump record by 21¾ inches in the Mexico Olympic Games. Moments where you ask yourself, 'did that just happen?'

It was at Old Trafford in 1993 when Shane Warne stepped up to bowl his first delivery in an Ashes Test. At the other end was Mike Gatting, renowned as a world-class player of spin bowling. Not content with a loosener, Warne delivered a spectacular ball which pitched several inches outside Gatting's leg stump. The batsman thrust his left leg at it, bat next to pad, knowing he could not be out LBW. The ball spun more than expected, passed the edge of the bat and clipped the top of off-stump. As journalist Martin Johnson put it at the time, 'How anyone can spin a ball the width of Gatting boggles the mind.'

Warne's earlier career had been less than spectacular and leg-spin, for many, was an antiquated art with little value and the potential to leak lots of runs. In an instant that all changed. Warne's career went from strength to strength within perhaps the greatest Test team of all. He showed that he had the ability to spin the ball yet keep control of the run-rate. Throughout much of his career he vied with Sri Lanka's Muttiah Muralitharan as the top bowler but it was great to see these two giving the old art a new popularity. With the doosra and suchlike spin bowling continues to evolve. Dear old Robin Hobbs must be watching on bemused as to how it has all happened. Just how much could he have made out of the modern game?

# 29  Doing the Double

The cricket season used to have a reassuring shape to it. The County Championship games would settle in over the weekend, with a rest day on Sunday, while the midweek slot was reserved for the Gillette Cup or Benson and Hedges competition. With no T20 or 50 over cricket there was plenty of opportunity for batsmen and bowlers to amass first-class runs and wickets. Batsmen would vie for the race to a thousand runs by the end of May. Few have made it. It is an exclusive club. WG Grace, Tom Hayward, Wally Hammond, Charlie Hallows, Don Bradman (twice), Bill Edrich, Glenn Turner and Graeme Hick are members. At a time when the weather can be dodgy, this has always been some achievement. Despite the restructuring towards white ball cricket, Nick Compton, James Hildreth and Joe Root have come close in recent years. Compton was denied by the weather when fifty runs short in 2012. It is doubtful that the club of eight will ever become nine. I wouldn't put money on it. In 2018, Yorkshire had just four Championship games before the end of May.

The ultimate all-round achievement was to score one thousand runs and take one hundred wickets in a season. The last time it was achieved in England was in 1988, by Franklyn Stephenson. Going into Nottinghamshire's last match, Stephenson had already got the wicket total but needed around two hundred runs to do the double. He slammed 111 and 117. Home in style and the first double since Nottinghamshire's Richard Hadlee four years previously. Just for good measure, Stephenson played golf to professional standard back home in Barbados. And so, the magic double has petered out. One-day matches do not count. The highest wicket taker in the 2017 County Championship was Essex's Jamie Porter with 75. Ten batsmen reached a thousand runs but none were frontline bowlers. What Stephenson and Hadlee achieved, therefore, was truly amazing but contrast that with years gone by. Yorkshire's Wilfred Rhodes completed the double sixteen times, his team-mate, George Hirst, fourteen around a century ago. That is truly startling.

For wicketkeepers, the totals were one thousand runs and one hundred dismissals. Only Les Ames (three times) and John Murray have managed that. These are statistics that have been well and truly consigned to history.

# 30 Favourite international cricketers

Many cricketers have emerged over the years. In the early days when my love of cricket was growing I would be fascinated by names, particularly from the sub-continent. There were many Indian and Pakistani cricketers with names almost lyrical in quality. The likes of Saeed Ahmed and Javed Burki would be introduced in my garden games and, of course, in 'Owzthat'. Imtiaz Ahmed, the Nawab of Pataudi and Hanif Mohammed were others who took their place in my batting line-ups solely on what they were called. Hanif, the 'Little Master', was famously run-out attempting his 500th run for Karachi against Bahawalpur. I never quite got that far in my games on the street. It was a first-class record that stood for more than 35 years until Brian Lara edged past in 1994. In this day and age, Hanif Mohammed would have made many more than his 55 Test appearances but Pakistan played much less international cricket back then.

Bishen Bedi was up there but I have extolled his virtues elsewhere. Mushtaq Mohammed was a magician, one of five brothers to play Test cricket for Pakistan, including Hanif. Mushtaq was a touch player, constantly twirling his bat at the crease and improvising. He was regarded as one of the first cricketers to use the reverse-sweep. 3643 Test runs at a shade under 40 represented not a bad return. On top of that he bowled leg breaks, googlies and flippers off a run up which came in from the direction of mid-off and had a bowling average of under 30. Between deliveries and even during the run-up 'Mushy' would constantly toss and spin the ball. He is in his mid-seventies now but I reckon he will still walk with a swagger and perform all sorts of magic with a piece of fruit before eating it for breakfast. He would have made a fortune in the T20 age, star of IPL, Big Blast and the rest.

I must have pretended to be Colin Bland for hours. A Test average of 49.08 for South Africa showed that he could bat and he was a useful medium-fast right-arm bowler but his lasting legacy lies as a fielder. He will go down in history as one of the greatest cover fielders. He had speed, balance and a wonderful throwing arm with a flat trajectory. That is what I mimicked as I played alone. Left-handed in my case but with a picture in my mind of an outstanding predator patrolling the off side. Bland's Test career lasted from 1961 to 1966 and was stunted by apartheid but he caught my imagination. I never saw him live but the television gave an indication of the sheer beauty of movement and power of delivery. I remember a demonstration he gave with one stump. He didn't let me down. That was how he had honed his skills and he would often show off his skills to the public during team fielding sessions. When Colin Bland was in his pomp, fielding standards were not as high as today. A fellow South African hurried it along thirty years after Bland. Jonty Rhodes. Like Bland, Rhodes was not a batsman who fielded. Nowadays with fielding coaches and fitness programmes the norm, standards have been driven up. Colin Bland would still have stood out and we could have witnessed his remarkable talents in all their glory through slo-mo replays from all angles. Ironically, his career ended in the field after a nasty collision with a boundary board badly damaged his left knee. It was a sad end for one of the greatest ever.

# 31  The Consummate County Cricketer

I admired Ken Suttle. I still do. He didn't play for my county but for one of those southern ones. Ken's was a career that would have suited me down to the ground. He was a Londoner who played for Sussex, primarily as a left-hand batsman but also a useful slow left-arm bowler. He was not the greatest cricketer Wisden ever featured. In fact, his career basically never went further than Sussex. But that is the basic point of my tribute. Ken Suttle was Mr. Consistency. He was the archetypal county cricketer, never quite good enough to play at international level. He played in 612 first-class matches between 1949 and 1971. That is some period. Just think how the world has changed in that time. Rationing, rock and roll, the Beatles, Kennedy was murdered, Man landed on the moon. Through all this and more there was one fixed constant.  Ken Suttle batted for Sussex. Between 1954 and 1969, there was an unbroken sequence of 423 county championship matches. I was born in the Summer of 1954. By 1969, I had stubble and was into Pink Floyd….. Just to ram home the point about steady Eddy. The average was nothing special. 31.09 with 49 centuries, bowling 32.8 with 266 wickets, 384 catches. It was good enough to keep that remarkable sequence going without quite being good enough to get an England call up. The closest was probably in the West Indies where he toured in 1953/54.

Ken Suttle

How many miles might he have covered during his career? From a home game at Hove up to the Scarborough Festival, out west to Gloucestershire. I wonder if his name was always first on the team sheet? Not a hero in the true sense of the word but a rewarding career. In a way, it's good that he never hit the big time because it makes that impression we have of him that bit more special.

# 32  A Wisden Schools Eleven 1974

Wisden is a total one-off. It is a thick, yellow-bound annual edition which is totally unique in sporting circles. The previous cricket year is covered in over fifteen hundred pages, such is the detail. There's a schools section which deals with the public and private sectors. It is tucked well away. In it you can scan the batting and bowling averages of players from the season before. Well, if you come across a copy from 1974 rummaging round in a junk shop you will find my name. I am on page 849, filed under Giggleswick School. To have my own small place in the iconic cricket book still means a lot. You needed 100 runs and ten wickets to make it and I got in for both. It was the school cricketer's version of doing the double. Giggleswick School had a good season in 1973. Seven wins and only two defeats from fifteen games was a pretty good record for a school our size. An asterisk next to my name indicates that I was captain. I averaged 17.22 with the bat, from thirteen innings with a top score of 24. Nothing special there. Four not outs helped the average. It was always nice to get a red-inker. My bowling looked better. I took thirty-five wickets at an average of 13.37 from nearly two hundred overs.

One rainy day my eye ran along the dozen Wisdens that occupy the top shelf of my bookcase devoted to cricket. I thought that it would be an interesting idea to see who else played in that mid-seventies season and indulge in that perennial favourite of cricket lovers-drawing up a team.

Well, I found a pretty decent team of players who also represented their school in that same summer. A tad short on bowling, admittedly, but it makes for an interesting group:

Chris Cowdrey (Tonbridge), Paul Downton (Sevenoaks), David Gower (Kings Canterbury), Matthew Fosh (Harrow),

Alistair Hignell (Denstone), Jeremy Lloyds (Blundell's), Vick Marks (Blundell's), Peter Roebuck (Millfield), Phil Slocombe (Millfield), Chris Tavare (Sevenoaks), Richard Le Quesne Savage (Marlborough)

With 126,781 first class runs between them I'd fancy my side with the bat. Wickets-wise they totalled 1261 but with 859 of those from Vic Marks it's likely he'll be trundling away from one end. It's a southern schools monopoly so you can imagine that I got nowhere near playing against any of these. The best the north could throw up for selection were Stephen Coverdale from St. Peter's, York and Peter Ingham and Peter Whiteley who all played for Yorkshire for a time. I couldn't find a more impressive stat than Chris Tavare's. The player who seemed to forget that scoring runs, preferably with style, was a batsman's priority, nay duty, took opposition attacks for 1036 runs at an average of 94.18. His top score was 164 not out. He was clearly more flamboyant back then. He would have to score some for my team because, looking down the list, I'm still worried about the bowling.

# 33 Cricket Pavilions

Pavilions come in all shapes and sizes and are the most evocative of places. It's the smells that hit you first. The three L's. Linament, linseed and leather. They seem to linger through the winter. Over the years teams have changed ready for battle, resolutely sticking to the same peg every week. Cricketers are creatures of habit. Woe betide you if you take the wrong peg on debut.

Pavilions are sites of former battles. They have resonated with the sounds of triumphs, disappointments and arguments. What stories could be told from within the four walls of the away dressing rooms at Headingley and Scarborough, where I had the honour of placing my cricket bag in the seventies and eighties? Who might have actually warmed the same bottom space that I did? Headingley's was side-on to the wicket at that time with the groundstaff and office personnel working underneath. Scarborough's has stayed resolutely in the same position between fine leg and square.

Traditional pavilions are architectural delights, timber-framed and often dating from Victorian times. There would be a balcony along the upper floor and invariably a clock above. These were common but they haven't all survived. There are many different lay outs these days. Sometimes, you are distant from your opponents, at other times too close for comfort. The vibes can put you off before you walk out on to the pitch. The confidence of a team in form can be unnerving. You have lost the toss, been inserted and as you strap your pads on waves of banter come through from next door. It is best not to listen too hard. 'You'll get another five-for against this lot, pal'. 'Just your type of wicket, mate. Wouldn't want to be facing you today.' There is an aura of supremacy that you just can't cope with. As you shuffle uneasily on your bench, a splinter enters your buttock. You just know that it isn't going to be your day.

# 34 Umpires

Umpires come in all shapes and sizes. There are the good, the bad and the bent. They hold the key to the success or otherwise of our eight hour trip away from wife and children on a Bank Holiday weekend. The previously-mentioned game example at Burnage in Manchester was a typical example. It was the furthest from home. Play started at three minutes past two and by four minutes past my day was over. LBW first ball off an inside edge.

Our life is in their hands and we will all remember those many times when the dreaded digit rises into the air to announce our departure from the crease. Equally, the many occasions when, as a bowler, an appeal to shake the foundations of the nearby houses is met with stony silence. Another coin is nonchalantly flicked from hand to hand. At a higher level there would be neutral umpires at both ends. Lower down, I've played in leagues where each team provides its own umpire every week. Players have even stood in at square leg. Then it gets interesting.

As skipper of Hull Zingari Second Team I was responsible for getting our umpire to home and away games. Staveley Belton was a former player at the club and captain himself. A lovely, lovely man, he lived on the avenues in Hull between the club and my school. Staveley was never in a rush so I allowed plenty of time. I would watch from a sumptuous armchair as he chose the match ball from the collection of used balls which he had carefully caressed and polished over the weeks. I'm sure his wife and family were a big part of Staveley's life but from where I was sitting no one could shower more love and affection as Staveley on his stock of cricket balls.

As an umpire, Staveley was not the perfect specimen. A former player of some repute but his LBW decisions could be controversial. It was at the end of the season when he exercised most power. He ran friendlies, by invitation only. There were two against Beverley, with a Driffield match sandwiched in between. Old cronies of his ran the opposition teams and I often waited patiently as he downed a few shorts with them in the pavilion. There was a ritual and tradition around Staveley's games. Nobody was ever invited twice. If you turned him down first time round you were never asked again. Players far better than I would ever be made that mistake and were subsequently discarded. He was a lovely man with an endearing chuckle but you didn't say 'No' to Staveley Belton.

There was a battle at Stamford Bridge in 1066 and many others in the seventies and eighties on the cricket field. I remember a season there in the second team when Staveley gave our captain out LBW. It didn't go down well with Sam, who had given him a lift to the game. After the match had finished both skipper and car had vanished. Staveley was left stranded.

There was another umpire in those East Yorkshire leagues who we reckon didn't give you out LBW if you had bought him a drink earlier in the season, your 'insurance' so to speak. I think he was a part-time lay preacher as well.

A friend remembers turning up one day to find an umpire dressed in plus-fours, cravat and jacket. He also had a shooting stick. Out he came with white coat on and proceeded to place his stick in the ground and sit on it. Some way into the game, the batsman swung a short ball round and hit it with some force straight towards square leg where the umpire was still sitting on the shooting stick. He had a second to get out of the way and failed. The ball hit him and he collapsed on the ground with a damaged back which meant an ambulance and a visit to hospital.

# 35 Scarborough in Winter

My wife and I celebrated a Roses partnership of forty years in 2018. I always reckoned I was pretty happy to reach forty when batting. As part of our Ruby celebrations we walked the length of the Yorkshire coastline (in stages) from the Tees to the Humber. Teesside was where we got married, Hull was where we lived in the early years. Unable to walk round the promenade in North Bay, due to a spectacularly high tide, we kept to higher ground. There was one thing on my mind and it was growing in size. I knew that we weren't far from Scarborough Cricket Club. I had not been there for a few years. Our route took us past the Scarborough Open Air Theatre, opened by the Queen, and the end of Peasholm Park, an attraction for holidaymakers since 1912. We gained height steadily along North Marine Road, passing hotels and guest houses where, for once, you would want a back room rather than a sea view. Turning right into the ground, I just hoped that the gates would be open. They were. There was a private party going on in the pavilion. It was cold and bleak and the ground was covered in frost but warm memories immediately flooded into my mind as I sat a few rows down on the Popular Bank. The cold did not seem to matter as I wallowed. Games played for Bradford and Hull Zingari vied for my attention with games watched. Seventeen years earlier I had crossed the north by train to watch Yorkshire win their first County Championship for thirty-three years. A sign above me pointed to Headingley, 69.1 miles away. It is still the main place but good on Yorkshire for keeping this evocative coastal ground on the fixture list.

Solitary at Scarborough

# 36  Taunton in Summer

My first visit to Taunton was in August 2018. My wife and I spent a few hours exploring the town as part of a holiday in Somerset. We drove in past the Cooper Associates County Ground and noticed a steady stream of punters heading to the cricket. Some wore obvious allegiance to Somerset who were at home to Essex in the County Championship Division One. The range of floppy headgear sported featured a number with the county's crest on the front. Coloured shirts bore both crest and name of sponsor. Official looking lanyards hung around a number of necks. Small rucksacks were carried. There was no chanting or disturbance. County cricket fans are a reserved bunch, happy to chat quietly to each other as they moved ever nearer. Many of these same people would have walked the same streets to watch Botham, Richards and Garner in the seventies and eighties. Those must have been exciting times.

I went back at around two thirty. Unwilling to pay £18 for half an hour (the car park stay was up after that) I did something that I have not done since childhood. A few yards from the car park entrance I was able to watch the play through the railings. The view offered half the playing area on the Sir Ian Botham Stand side and I was just unable to see the batsman at the near end but I settled in for an absorbing period of cricket right up my street. Somerset had Essex in some trouble. Half their wickets had fallen for little over a hundred, chasing 324. Bowling in tandem were two of England's finest young spinners, Jack Leach and Dom Bess. Left-armer Leach was born and raised in Taunton and used to be employed parking trolleys at a nearby branch of Sainsbury's. Bess the off-spinner is Devonian by birth. Both have attracted much attention for their performances in recent seasons. As England struggled in the Test at Trent

Bridge it was good to watch some old-fashioned cricket with two young spinners grinding the Essex batsmen down. Wickets fell steadily with only Ryan ten Doeschate offering any resistance. There was a decent crowd and this iconic ground looked a picture. It was a passage of play for the purist in front of a holiday crowd of some size. Who says that the County Championship is on its last legs?

Peeping through the railings at Taunton

What I saw neatly summed up much of my cricketing life and memories came flooding back from childhood onwards. It was somehow appropriate that two spinners, my most favourite of cricketers, should have centre stage on a cricket ground steeped in history and in a competition that symbolises much of what this great sport means to me. All I needed was a bottle of Dandelion and Burdock and my joy would have been complete.